When You
Lose Your
JOB

When You
Lose Your
JOB

Laid Off • Fired • Early Retired
Relocated • Demoted • Unchallenged

Cliff Hakim

Berrett-Koehler Publishers
San Francisco

Berrett-Koehler Publishers, Inc.
155 Montgomery Street
San Francisco, CA 94104–4109

Ordering Information
Orders by individuals and organizations. Berrett-Koehler publications are available through bookstores or can be ordered direct from the publisher at the Berrett-Koehler address above or by calling (800) 929–2929.

Quantity sales. Berrett-Koehler publications are available at special quantity discounts when purchased in bulk by corporations, associations, and others. For details, write to the "Special Sales Department" at the Berrett-Koehler address above or call (415) 288–0260.

Orders by U.S. trade bookstores and wholesalers. Please contact Publishers Group West, 4065 Hollis Street, Box 8843, Emeryville, CA 94608; tel. (800) 788–3123; fax (510) 658–1834.

Orders for college textbook/course adoption use. Please contact Berrett-Koehler Publishers, 155 Montgomery Street, San Francisco, CA 94104–4109; tel. (415) 288–0260; fax (415) 362–2512.

Printed in the United States of America

Printed on acid-free and recycled paper that meets the strictest state and U.S. guidelines for recycled paper (50 percent recycled waste, including 10 percent postconsumer waste).

Library of Congress Cataloging-in-Publication Data
Hakim, Cliff, 1951–
 When you lose your job : laid off, fired, early retired,
relocated, demoted, unchallenged / Cliff Hakim. — 1st ed.
  p.   cm.
 ISBN 1-881052-25-7 (paper); $14.95
 1. Unemployment—Psychological aspects. 2. Underemployment—
Psychological aspects. 3. Job hunting. 4. Career development.
 I. Title.
HD5708.H35 1993
331.13′7′019—dc20   93-2707
                                                              CIP

FIRST EDITION
First Printing 1993

To Amy, for her love and support and for learning with me
To my mother and my father

Contents

Career/Job Transition Tools

Preface

We have all heard "timing is everything." This age old adage seems to hold some truth in most of what we do: meeting our spouse, making a prudent investment, or closing a competitive sale. Currently, job loss is affecting the lives of millions. Jobs and work, once core to this country's development and the well-being of every worker, can no longer be guaranteed. Now is the time for all of us to take control of our jobs and careers before, as well as after, job loss occurs.

WHY I WROTE THIS BOOK

I wrote *When You Lose Your Job* for three reasons. The first was as a way of reflecting what I was hearing in the job marketplace. In my career consulting practice, as I listened to and coached people in career transition, I began to hear a new language. For example, people would use phrases such as "Can I tell you my story?" "Can you help me express my true self?" "I need to heal." and "Is it okay not to have all the answers?" This language expressed the need for deeper self-clarification and renewal and for finding more meaningful work. Simply listing one's skills, surveying the marketplace, sending out resumés, and then waiting for an employer to call was not only no longer working, it was no longer personally gratifying. These experiences gave birth to the basic content of the book.

I also wrote this book as means of self-expression, as part of my own cathartic transition and reconnection to what I wanted: meaningful and challenging work. After more than three years of painful debate, I closed my successful placement and search firm. I laid myself off because I was feeling unchallenged and wanted something more. Earning a good income and looking successful became secondary to the renewal of my spirit. The price of this choice has been living with confusing times, uncertainty, and hard work. A sense of clarity, feeling good about who I am and what I do are my rewards.

Finally, I wrote this book as a message to you. You can make a choice. If you stick with your choice, your dream will come true. I chose to write this book in a different way — a story form. By using my creative voice, I believe I can add value to your life and mine. Most career-related books are written in a traditional "how to" format, with lists and recipes on what needs to be done. I felt that changed times, these times, called for a different strategy based on the ability to "tell stories" — detailed narratives of what you've done, where you've been, who you are, and what you'll be able to do. Listing your abilities and skills is no longer enough. Employers and customers want to know *you,* and they want to know *what you can do for them.* I encourage you to make a choice. Use your creativity. Tell your story. It works!

HOW TO READ THIS BOOK

First, read this book as you would any other story — from cover to cover. If you're so inclined, read it in one or two sittings. Alternatively, read it chapter by chapter, in between discussing the ideas presented with your spouse, friends, associates, or someone else who is in career transition.

"When You Lose Your Job," the poem on page xvii, encapsulates what you most need to know and do. During your transition, refer to it for guidance and inspiration.

The first three chapters validate your feelings and give you some practical suggestions for expressing your emotions, finding support, dealing with your finances, and determining first steps. Chapters 4 through 7 help you rethink your strategy, gain focus, network, name your skills and values, and develop tools for negotiating the marketplace. Chapters 8 through 10 guide you through your "outer work": writing your resumé and marketing letter, selling yourself and interviewing, getting back on track when the going gets tough, and saying thank you to everyone who helped. Chapter 11, "Going Beyond," is meant to encourage you to deepen your learning and prepare you for the continuation of your journey. Finally, the resource and reference chapter suggests books, directories, support groups, and other resources for managing job loss, job search, and "going beyond."

After you've read through the story, this book becomes a practical guide, with helpful suggestions, such as "Ten Commandments for Winning Interviews," and tools, such as "Life, Inc.," you can refer to and use at any time throughout your journey. These tools and suggestions will become essential elements of the continuous practice necessary for achieving your goals.

ACKNOWLEDGMENTS

Writing this book began as an idea, progressed into several periods of solitary thought and writing, and then evolved as a team effort. I'd like to acknowledge and thank "my team" for their support, feedback, ideas, and encouragement.

First, I'd like to thank all the job seekers and career changers who shared their feelings, hardships, discoveries, and successes with me.

I'd like to thank Berrett-Koehler Publishers: Steven Piersanti, president, for "building castles in the air and foundations under them"; Patricia Anderson, marketing director, for her creative insights and risk taking; Val Barth, publicity and promotion manager, for her worldly perspectives; also Valerie McOuat, director of business and administration, Kristen Scheel, sales manager, Mark Carstens, office administrator, and Stephen Zink, operations administrator, for their expertise and vitality. My thanks to the team for their commitment to this project and for doing business in a supportive way—for truly "practicing what they preach."

As well, I'd like to express my gratitude to Evelyn Mercer Ward and John R. Ward of Trinity Publishers Services for their expertise and teamwork—editing and producing this book.

In addition, I'd like to express my appreciation to Julie Hoey, for the cover illustration and for reminding me to "keep on the same track and do what your heart tells you—it's right"; David Robinson, for believing in a good idea and making it better; Dr. Vincent Calia, for his spirit and invaluable story telling; Andrea Szmyt, for her inspiration and friendship and for wishing me "a piece of the action"; Penny Barrows, for what she taught me about loving work; Perry Constas, for his optimism, honesty, and openness to learning; Suanne Williams-Lindgren, for her gracious and constructive suggestions about the manuscript; Nancy Fulford, for her friendship and for lighting candles; Dr. Gardner Yenawine, Jane McHale, and Bob Ginn, for their teachings, which have been used and tested; John Willig, for being a reasonable unreasonable man; Irving Sands, for the constant reminder to "believe in yourself"; Bruce Albert, for reminding me to go back to the beginning; John Shibley, for his confidence that "lead can be transmuted into gold"; Roger Drumm, for recognizing a labor of love; Lynn Robinson, for listening and encouraging; and Casey Sims, for her attention to the details.

Finally, my thanks to everyone who read the manuscript for giving me invaluable feedback.

Cambridge, Massachusetts   Cliff Hakim
February 1993

The Author

CLIFF HAKIM is a career consultant and coach who believes that organizations are only as good as the individuals within them. Individuals do their best for themselves and their organizations when their work is firmly aligned with their values, career plan, and the system's needs. Hakim works with people in an organization to make this happen. His organization consulting practice includes *Fortune* 500 corporations, professional service firms, universities, and associations.

Hakim (pronounced Ha-*keem*) provides the same service for individuals who are in transition outside the organization. His individual client practice includes professionals and managers at all levels who are seeking guidance for job and/or career change. Clients range from firm partners to human resource managers to fast-track business executives.

Hakim earned his master's degree in special education from Boston College and has done postgraduate work in human and organization development at the Fielding Institute. Several of his articles on career-/work-related issues have been published in professional and national magazines, such as *HRMagazine* and *National Business Employment Weekly*. He is a frequent speaker on career issues.

For the past several years, Hakim has been deeply interested in the subject of how people progress in their work and enhance their careers under varying conditions. One area of particular interest to him is job loss — specifically, what people go through when they lose their jobs and how they turn despair into opportunity. *When You Lose Your Job* is an outgrowth of his personal journey and professional practice. An up-to-date, practical, and supportive story, this book is filled with information, tools, and rich philosophy. It is meant to help people take charge of job transition by dealing with their feelings, focusing their energies, and making choices that can turn crisis into opportunity. The book is also about learning—lifelong learning that involves viewing the loss of a job, transitioning between jobs, and beginning a new job as parts of a learning continuum—namely, life.

The author welcomes your comments, questions, and conversation and invites you to contact him at Hakim and Company, 55 Wheeler Street, Cambridge, MA 02138, 617-661-1250 (FAX 617-868-3462).

When You Lose Your Job

Easy does it. You're not to blame.

Talk with others. You'll need the support.

Don't panic. It's okay not to have all the answers.

Your feelings are normal. "I'm scared" is temporary.

Ask for support. It feels good.

Tell your story. You'll gain confidence and become clear.

Go step by step. You'll learn new skills.

Trust yourself. You'll learn how.

Listen. You'll learn a lot.

Persevere. You'll overcome obstacles.

Stay flexible. Change will become easier.

Step back. You'll see things more clearly.

Contact others. You'll discover opportunities.

Give a contact. Someone gave you one.

Make plans. You'll meet your goals.

Take action. You'll get results.

Express yourself. Don't just play to the audience.

Take chances. You'll have everything to gain.

Say thank you. You'll never be forgotten.

Go beyond. Deepen your learning.

Introduction

Job loss is not going away. The companies we trusted — Wang Laboratories, Digital Equipment Corporation, Siemens-Nixdorf, and Aetna Life & Casualty, to name just a few — have laid off thousands of workers at all levels. Projections show that these companies will continue laying off workers as world economies merge, collaborate, and compete. The ebb and flow of jobs in smaller companies is not as dramatic or as public, but believe me — or ask your neighbor — it's there. Many of the employees who remain in their jobs are also hurting, waiting for an opportunity to get out or wondering if they'll be kicked out. Today, no one's job is secure.

By now, it is likely that every one of us knows someone who has lost his or her job; some of us know several. You, in fact, may be one. The following are statements of your fellow workers — laid off, fired, early retired, relocated, demoted, and unchallenged:

> We were manufacturing outmoded technology . . . the competition was killing us. We could no longer pour money into a sink hole. I was caught in the company's first massive layoff, about 5,000 and more to come.
>
> Engineer (laid off)

> I was the first human resource manager that the company had ever hired. Initially I thought and they thought we had a good match. It was a four-year roller coaster ride. They didn't want to change. . . . I became a victim.
>
> Human resource manager (fired)

1

I read about other companies dumping middle management, but it seemed that we were safe. Not a chance, the company was holding on, telling us not to worry. We had two miserable quarters in a row. Next thing we knew, veterans, managers with more than fifteen, twenty years, were getting a choice: stay on and see what happens, or take a one-time offer. At fifty-two, I took early retirement.

Operations manager (early retired)

Like many professionals during the eighties, I took advancement for granted. If I kept my nose to the grindstone, I'd get my pay increase and climb another rung. Let me tell you, traditional career ladders are defunct!

Senior marketing manager (demoted)

Is the day over yet? Increasingly, my gut would churn . . . every day. I got paid big bucks for creating the ads that helped pollute our world. With the support of a counselor, I affirmed my priorities, which led me to working out a severance agreement with my employer. I left with my values, looking for a new challenge.

Vice president of public relations (unchallenged)

Lost jobs, an uncertain future, and the feelings of loss—shock, betrayal, fear, denial, anger, and relief—interconnect all of these individuals in a radically changed global marketplace. All will need to learn new skills, and sharpen others, to find jobs. Many will be required to change careers or invent new ones. Skills development will not only involve those skills necessary for transition and job search—expressing feelings, problem solving, planning, networking, and interviewing, to name a few—but also specific professional skills. These will be the skills for which employers and customers will pay.

In the eighties, many professionals and job seekers latched onto the corporate career ladder. The direction was up, and the path was narrow. With increased global competition and organizational restructuring, the "rungs," or positions, of this ladder have become worn, broken, or obsolete. Corporate structures have shifted, no longer able to support multiple-tiered career ladders. Instead, companies must think, plan, and act in ways that get the job done simply and directly meet customer needs. Many organizations that were growing feverishly in the eighties—IBM, Citibank, Amoco—have downsized, are rethinking strategy, and are hiring fewer employees in reaction to a changing world. Because we are in a whole new "ball game," we must learn to think and act differently and to express and use our feelings, particularly those that can help facilitate our mobility. This book will teach you how to do this.

We are witnessing and experiencing a global socioeconomic shift that impacts most Americans and our world neighbors. This shift is altering how we work, where we work, and when we work and has significantly affected the confidence of this nation's workers. Not only are workers at the blue-collar level losing their jobs, but, as never before, white-collar workers and those in between are also facing major dilemmas. No one is exempt. The finance, real estate, computer technology, and retail sectors have been greatly affected. When current jobs lost are added to those that have been lost, a critical picture develops. Factors such as saturated markets, global competition, and reduced consumer spending have resulted in massive change. *When You Lose Your Job* was written to give people who have lost their jobs, and those who might, the hope and courage to negotiate through personal change and a changed marketplace—to do their best in these times and go beyond. The book is intended as a guide for self-renewal and espouses practical tools and an empowering philosophy based on continuous learning, creativity, and self-management.

When You Lose Your Job emerged out of the process of talking and exploring options with people who had been laid off, fired, early retired, demoted, or unchallenged. The book explores a viable option for career mobility called the "lattice approach." The *Oxford American Dictionary* defines *lattice* as a framework of crossed "laths," or bars, with the spaces between used as a screen or fence. The now-defunct career ladder can be redefined as a *career lattice,* a structure supporting different paths, each one involving career choices based on skills, values, interests, and marketplace research. A career lattice provides many options that a career ladder cannot. A career ladder suggests that there are only two ways to go: up or down. Up usually meant success; and down . . . well, most of us tried to avoid that. The lattice approach offers many more options, allowing the latitude to move in any direction — to either side, as well as up or down.

Although the event used to illustrate the lattice approach in this book is a layoff, the lattice approach is applicable to other forms of job change — fired, early retired, relocated, demoted, or unchallenged — as well as to those who are choosing to get off the "fast track." In *The Popcorn Report,* Faith Popcorn* refers to this trend as "cashing out." Explaining that "in the eighties, we lived to work. Now we simply want to live — long and well. It's [cashing out] not copping out or dropping out or selling out. It's cashing in career chips you've been stacking up all these years, and going somewhere else to work at something you want to do, the way you want to do it."

Matthew, the protagonist in *When You Lose Your Job,* is a mid-level manager who has been laid off from a high-tech company. At forty-seven, Matthew decides he will not settle for second best, even in a fiercely competitive market fraught with downsizing and restructuring. Instead, he determines to do what is necessary to achieve his goal of finding meaningful work — namely, to take responsibility for his career search. Matthew learns that the boundaries of the traditional career ladder are too narrow for achieving his goal in an unpredictable, changing marketplace, so instead he chooses a career lattice approach, following up many different paths to more worthy employment. During this sometimes painful and discouraging but also challenging and exciting period of his life, Matthew discovers the tools of successful job transition: tell your story; express and sort out your feelings; confront your own and others' expectations; know your core skills, values, and interests; demonstrate your skills and values by giving concrete examples; and do in-depth marketplace research.

Throughout this process, he learns to stay flexible, realizing that the ultimate point of finding a good "fit" in a job depends on showing how he can add value to the customer or company.

Pursuing and negotiating successful career transition requires both "inner work" and "outer work." *Learning* and *action* thus become the crucial elements that lead to meaningful work.

*Faith Popcorn, *The Popcorn Report* (New York: Doubleday, 1991), 50–55.

Over the past several years, in my position as a career consultant I have been approached by many job seekers who have begun looking for a job or career change by writing and sending out resumés. To their dismay, their initial efforts proved futile. This is because a resumé that works must be based on the clarification of one's skills, values, interests, and career objective. As Matt's journey illustrates, in today's market, flooded with hundreds of resumés per job, other job-search methods can be more effective. These outer manifestations are powerful tools only when an individual has done the important "inner work" first. "Inner work" represents those areas of development (personality, values, and attitude) that require more internal examination. "Outer work" refers to those concerns (such as finances, networking, and interviewing) that are more external to the search process. In the lattice approach discussed in this book, internal and external processes operate simultaneously. Like the growth of a tree, as the core receives nutrients, new bark, limbs, and leaves take form.

As with Matt, those who have been most successful finding jobs and recreating their careers have done so by using a lattice approach. They have focused on a two-part process of learning and action. Through this process they have renewed their energy, clarified their skills, researched the marketplace, and found jobs.

Job transition is a complex and challenging process. Matthew's personal reactions and encounters as he progresses through this life passage are ones that all who have had similar experiences will resonate to and learn from.

1

Time Out

Easy does it

Tuesday, February 23, my phone rang at two o'clock. It was Mr. Carroll, my boss at Technology, Inc., a computer manufacturer that had been bought by a large conglomerate seven months before. "Matt," intruded Mr. Carroll, "will you meet me at my office at about 3:30?"

"Today?" I asked.

"Of course today, I would have said tomorrow if I meant tomorrow," snapped Mr. Carroll. Click. That was the end of that. Hardly a conversation, as usual.

Mr. Carroll had been my boss and the vice president of manufacturing for five months. He was one of those fast trackers in his late thirties who was chosen by the parent company to oversee restructuring because of his reputation as a turnaround manager. He hadn't made very many friends, but he was noted for making decisions. In the past couple of months, he had laid off forty employees, mostly blue-collar, and had reduced inventory by about 19 percent. Behind his back he was known as "Mr. Control." Everything and everyone to him was a "controllable expense."

For some reason I felt reluctant about this meeting, but I thought, why should this be different from any other? He probably wanted me to crack down on employees who were getting to work late or were taking an extended lunch hour.

"Matt, how are you?" said Mr. Carroll. He gestured to take a seat. As I sat, I responded, "Feeling pretty well."

"That's good," he said. There was a pause and Mr. Carroll began to tap the side of his thumb on the desk. He continued, "You know, the business climate looks pretty bleak, and we've got to run things lean around here."

"How do you mean?" I asked.

"Well, let me be direct. We've got too many high-level people running manufacturing," he said. I could feel my shoulders stiffen, my jaw tighten, my feet trying to grip the floor.

"I'm having to make some tough decisions, Matt. One of them is to let you go. To lay you off. Sorry," he said, leaning back in his chair and avoiding my eyes. The rest of the conversation was a blur.

I was stunned. I felt betrayed. I mumbled, "I can't believe it, I don't believe this." I eased myself out of the chair and walked, with my head down, back to my office. Everything seemed different to me. I closed the door and sat thinking about the callous look on Mr. Carroll's face. I shook my head in disbelief that this office was no longer mine. Where was I going to go? What was I going to do? It had been tough enough getting a job when I was younger. What was it going to be like now?

To this point in my career, I'd worked about twenty-five years on staff and as a manager in manufacturing and high-tech companies — long enough to have moved from a role as order taker to decision maker. Years ago, when I first started in the field, I'd hired, fired, made sure deadlines were met, and oriented new employees. I began as an individual contributor, worked with four different organizations, and at Technology, Inc., was promoted to senior line manager.

Generally, my role in management evolved into a more integral part of organization productivity. My colleagues and I had progressed to working in the areas of employee relations, policy interpretation, staff selection, and total quality management. Quite a change from the old days! At the same time, I had less control of my own destiny, no matter how hard I worked. I felt my role as a manager had little to do with steering the direction of the organization, no matter what the extent of my company loyalty.

Frustrating! As these signs and my intuition reminded me, I could be "let go" any time.

During the past several years, there was an air of distrust, not only in my company, but also throughout corporate America. Layoffs occurred for several reasons. Sometimes an organization, impeded by increased competition, corporate takeover, or inability to pay back debt, could no longer support its overhead. As more organizations dismissed employees with the purpose of running more efficiently, one significant result was fewer jobs in corporate America. This all seemed to make some sense.

Even though I had thought about being laid off, emotionally I was hit hard. I guess being told, "Matthew, you're not needed" is never easy. During my career I had laid off others. Now I knew what it felt like.

I left the office, avoiding eye contact with anyone. On the way home, my head felt thicker than the traffic. For now, all I could remember were the words "laid off" and Mr. Carroll's tapping thumb. "I'll have to let you go, to lay you off." Those words sat in my stomach like pieces of lead.

"You look awful," exclaimed Lynda, my wife. She put her hands on my arms and tilted her head for a better look.

"I'll be all right," I muttered. Lynda guided me over to the wingback chair, and I flopped into the seat.

"What's wrong?" she asked.

"Mr. Carroll let me go. I was laid off. Aggh . . . tomorrow is my last day." Lynda held my left hand with both of hers. She said nothing for about thirty seconds. I could feel the comfort of her touch and also the thickness in my head.

My eyes met hers and she said, "I don't know what we're going to do, but we'll be fine. We'll figure things out."

"I'm not sure. I feel awful. I just need to sit for a while."

I've been married to Lynda for twenty-three years. We've been through our ups and downs, with the help of about three years of couples therapy interspersed throughout our marriage. Lynda is energetic and is generally more flexible and less intense than I, and she's often the one to put things in perspective. For example, if I plan too many things for one day, she'll say, "Matt, relax, take a break. Rome wasn't built in a day."

The Job/Career Ladder

That evening, Lynda called George, my psychologist friend, whom I had met at a marathon about ten years ago. George is a very accepting friend. He's got nothing to prove, and he's comfortable just being himself. We've had miles of conversation during our weekly runs.

"Lynda, you sound alarmed," said George. "What's wrong?"

"Well, Matt came home upset today. It's hard to believe, but he's been laid off. He lost his job."

"I'm really sorry to hear that, Lynda."

"The changes in the economy have hit *our* home."

"Mmm, I can see that. What is Matt doing now?"

"He's sitting in his chair having tea."

"Well, it's good that he's relaxing. Lynda, take care. If you want to talk, please call."

"I'll get Matt."

As Lynda was talking with George, I was thinking that I didn't feel like talking with anyone, not even George. I just felt like hibernating, hoping that when I woke up I'd have my job back.

"Matt, how are you?"

"Awful. I feel strange—thick and numb. Like Lynda said, they let me go today."

"I'm sorry. That must have been a shock."

"Yeah," I said. "I got the usual discourteous call from Mr. Carroll asking if I could meet with him at 3:30. I thought it was going to be routine matters—but I got the same boot as the other employees."

"That's tough. . . . How about a run tomorrow morning?"

"All right. See you in the morning, about 6:30."

I had a fitful sleep, but the next morning the cold air felt good as we ran along the woodland trail. My steps felt heavy, even though I knew we were running close to our regular speed. Thank God, I thought, at least I have running, Lynda, and my friend George to rely on.

As we settled into our pace, I turned to George for some answers. "George, yesterday I felt out of it, like I was in shock. Today I feel numb and scared. What do you think is going on?"

"I'll try to explain. You were in shock yesterday," George replied. "And you'll feel different degrees of shock as you come to understand the impact of losing your job."

"I think I know what you mean," I answered. "This feeling reminds me of when I've cut myself badly. You know what I mean?"

"Not exactly."

"Just after I cut myself I can see physically what has happened, but I don't yet feel the pain."

"That's a good example. Your numb response is a form of protection. It's like a buffer zone against too much stress related to loss."

"Mmmm, I guess."

"Have you heard of Elizabeth Kübler Ross?"

"I think so."

George continued, "In her book, *On Death and Dying,** she defined the grieving process after the loss of a loved one. People who lose their jobs go through similar stages of loss."

"What are they?"

"Shock or denial, depression and often anger, acceptance, and resolution. It's important not to overreact when you're in shock. Try to take it easy — do some running, relax, and talk with good friends."

"I'll try. I've been working too hard to just relax."

We hurdled a log, and George responded, "I mean, don't go and start looking for a job tomorrow. First, you've got to sort some things out."

I mumbled, "Mr. Carroll, that S.O.B."

"I can see why you'd blame your boss. Blaming is often one of our reactions when we've lost something that was special to us. Matt, this is a tough one. Remember, I'll listen when you need an ear."

"Yeah, thanks . . . If it wasn't for him."

We continued in silence up the hill for about half a mile, then I said, "What about the acceptance stage?"

"That's when you gain understanding of what happened. During this last stage is when you'll probably find a job. Hopefully, the one you want."

Well into our fifth mile, I was starting to feel nauseous. I focused on finishing, nothing more. As we approached my house, George stopped before going on to his. He put his hand on my shoulder and said, "Good luck today. Call tonight if you'd like to talk."

I was confused. My head was saying, Thank God for the support; accept it. But the rest of me wanted to retreat, to talk to no one, to feel bad for myself.

My nausea had subsided, although the coffee didn't smell very good as I opened the door. Lynda had already left for school.

*Elizabeth Kübler Ross, *On Death and Dying* (New York: Macmillan, 1969).

She teaches English at the high school and volunteers at a local art collaborative, where she sells her pottery.

Under my cup, Lynda had left a note.

Honey, I'm sorry this has happened. I know we'll be fine. Most important, take care of yourself today.
                                        Love,
                                        Lynda

I turned to our cat, August, and said, "That's my Lynda." Too bad, I thought, that August can't talk . . . but at least she listens pretty well!

I got dressed as usual—sport coat, white shirt, and a colorful tie—and was promptly at work by 8:30. On the inside I was still feeling thick and heavy, but I wouldn't show this to Mr. Carroll and his cohort.

"Sorry, Matt," said Mike Fielder, one of the other managers, who I considered a buddy. "Yeah, me too," I responded. "This isn't easy, but I'll be okay."

Mike responded, with a knowing look in his eyes, "Matt, we'll miss ya."

"Thanks, the feeling's mutual."

Leaning toward me, he said, "Frankly, I don't trust this place anymore. I hate to admit it, but who knows, I might be next. For now, I'm going to get involved in that new project and start to look around."

"You mean look for another job?"

"That's it. I've got to face that I could end up without a job, and I've been here longer than you."

"I think you're right to cover your bases."

"That's reality these days. Isn't it, Matt?"

"Yup . . . I've got to go. See you around."

"This isn't good-bye, just so long."

I spent the morning visiting some of the managers, supervisors, and other employees, basically saying good-bye. Many of them had a tough time facing me, as if I was a reminder that this could happen to them and they needed to shield themselves. For example, one of the supervisors wished me well and said, "They

can't touch my job — the project I'm working on is too important. Besides, they couldn't run it without me." I just nodded.
As painful as saying good-bye was, I needed to.

"Matt!" my name was yelled from a distance.

"Yeah," I responded, before completely turning to see who it
was. I could feel myself tensing as Mr. Carroll approached. Stand
erect, I reminded myself, remain calm, and stay positive.

"I've arranged for you to talk with Ron Law, the director of
human resources, at one o'clock. Ron will explain your severance and any other questions you might have."

"Okay."

As we both began to turn, Mr. Carroll extended his hand.
"Good luck, Matt."

I thought, This guy thinks he's Mr. Invincible. He hasn't been
knocked off his horse *yet*. I patted myself on the back for keeping my composure. Even though I was angry, it never pays to
burn a bridge. Mr. Carroll couldn't find a reason to fault me for
my work, why give him any excuse on my way out?

"Matt, I was expecting you. Have a seat," said Ron Law. Ron
was the new director of human resources brought in by the parent company. This was our second face-to-face meeting. "How
are you?"

"Fine, considering." I thought, How does he think I am?

"You know," said Ron, "the measures we've been taking to
cut staff are purely business decisions. Performance and personality aren't the factors here. We're in a downturn and simply have
too many people on the payroll."

For a moment I felt despair. There seemed to be no bargaining. My position was being eliminated.

I eked out the words, "I understand." I figured I'd try to keep
Ron as an ally.

The word *downturn* triggered a thought. In one of my books
on management, I remembered reading a statement by the chairman of Honda Motors. If I recall, he said, "American management's answer to a downturn in business is the layoff." I gazed
out the window and cracked a slight smile, thinking I'm not to
blame, nor am I alone.

Ron pulled some papers out of the side file of his desk. When

---

Time Out

Do's and Don'ts

DO . . .

- Negotiate for a severance.
- Part on good terms with your boss and colleagues.
- Collect names and phone numbers of colleagues who could be supportive in the future.
- Realize it's normal to feel shocked.
- Contact at least one person who will *listen*. Talk about your feelings.
- Keep part of your daily routine. Exercise—walk, run, play tennis, and so on.

DON'T . . .

- Burn any bridges.
- Pretend nothing has happened.
- Try to figure out everything at once.
- Use your energy to squelch your feelings.
- Stagnate.
- Isolate yourself.
- Abuse anybody because of the way you feel.

---

he looked up, he reminded me of Mr. Carroll. He began, "We're giving you the same package as we would all managers at your level—that is, four months' full pay with benefits."

"Four months?"

"Yes. That's the best we can do."

My throat tightened, and I gulped. I began to say, "It's a tough . . ." then thought better about continuing. Ron knows it's a tough job market, but probably figures that's not his problem. What's most important is to follow the rules.

I left early that day, at three o'clock. It hadn't sunk in yet, but that moment ended almost five years with Technology, Inc.

I was being forced to change during these times — tough times.

2

Don't Panic

It's okay not to have all the answers

I awoke the next morning at six, my usual time. Something was wrong. Why hadn't the alarm clock gone off? Then it all came flooding back to me. There was no need to get up early this morning. There was no need to go into the office. There was no eight o'clock staff meeting—not for me. I had been laid off.

As my drowsiness cleared, I began to count my losses—a community of work colleagues, a familiar commute, prestige, a work culture I understood, programs that I'd put into place, the security guard's smile, travel to other company sites, and welcome financial rewards and company benefits. Without them, what was I? Who was I?

I tried to console myself; at least I was no longer a survivor, like so many of my former colleagues. They were still victims, feeling trapped in an uncertain and changing system. I had now moved on. Now I was free. Or was I? Physically I was free, but emotionally I was feeling confused—still part of Technology, Inc. How could I survive on the outside?

Within me, a voice said, "Don't panic. It's okay not to have all the answers. You're still a good and productive person."

After breakfast, as I finished my coffee, I decided my first call would be to an accountant friend, Russ. As difficult as it was for me to ask for help, during times of crisis, I have learned to get to the practical — quickly. Russ was a good listener, and I needed his help to develop a temporary financial plan. Thank God I'd been given four full months' severance pay! I'd heard that as more organizations restructure, it's taking longer — six to eighteen months — to find a job that's a good match.

Just to hear Russ's voice was calming.

"Russ, have you straightened out that golf swing yet? This is Matt."

"Matt, I'd know that voice anywhere. Besides, only you know what a great golfer I am! What's up? How are you?"

"Well, Russ," I began, "I'm calling this time with lousy news. I've been laid off. I was told on Tuesday, and I left for good yesterday."

"Aw, gee. Sorry to hear that, Matt," he replied. "Anything I can do to help?"

"I'm glad you asked. This is a tough situation. I could use your help to take an objective look at my cash flow."

"You mean you'd like me to help you set up a financial plan?"

"Exactly."

"How about Monday afternoon?" Russ suggested. "Bring Lynda along. You'll be able to manage things better together. You know, two problem solvers are better than one."

"Thanks, Russ, good idea. We'll see you Monday at two."

"Monday it is."

Looking out the kitchen window, I thought, Russ is one of those guys I really trust. That was a good suggestion to include Lynda.

Even though I didn't much feel like it, and I was concerned about finances, we kept our social plans for the weekend. Saturday night we had dinner out with David and Maggie Clark, a younger couple in their mid thirties. David and Maggie had bought a few pieces of Lynda's pottery through the artists' collaborative. During dinner, Maggie commented, "Your pottery is the perfect complement for our living room."

Lynda smiled and said, "Thank you. It's nice to hear that you're enjoying my work."

I wasn't much in the mood for conversation, so I mostly listened. I was just glad to be out. Otherwise, I'd probably have been at home stewing. Fortuately, no one seemed to notice.

Over dessert, David said, "Maggie and I haven't taken an extended vacation in over two years. We're thinking about going camping and hiking this summer."

Maggie looked out the window at the view. Lynda's eyes followed, and she said, "The simplest vacations are the best—fun and inexpensive."

David replied, "Yes, we've thought about the White Mountains. Also possibly flying to Yellowstone. We've got some investigating to do."

I added, "Air fares are volatile these days. I'd keep my eyes open for a reasonable rate."

"Good idea," Maggie replied.

All the while, I'd been thinking that Lynda and I would probably have to forego our vacation to the West Coast. Thus far I hadn't mentioned being laid off to Maggie and David, and I didn't plan to. I wasn't ready to make my situation known.

We split the check. Even half of the bill, severance or not, was a bitter reminder of money going out.

As I shook David's hand, I said, "Good seeing you. Your vacation plans sound great."

"Thank you, we're looking forward to it. Take care, Matt."

Lynda turned to me as we strolled toward our car. "You didn't say much all evening."

"I wasn't feeling so hot, especially when David began talking about vacations."

"What do you mean?"

"Well, with my situation I'm uneasy about spending money to go anywhere. I know we have savings and I have four months' severance, but we'll have to adjust—I can't predict how long it will take me to find a job."

"Matt, I was counting on seeing my family this spring! I've told them we're coming."

"Lynda, take it easy."

I was silent for a moment as I unlocked the passenger door. Walking around to the driver's side I thought, I hate to disappoint her, but I'm not working.

Lynda continued as I maneuvered out of the parking space, "You mentioned to Maggie and David that they're likely to get a cheap fare right now!"

"They're both working."

"You've got four months' pay coming."

"Okay, okay, let's wait and talk with Russ on Monday. We'll see what he has to say."

Lynda looked relieved. "Thanks, Matt. Thanks for listening."

I felt that lead in my stomach and thickness in my head again. I turned to Lynda and said, "This isn't easy. Please be patient."

I didn't mention exactly how I felt. I wasn't used to these feelings and didn't want to worry her needlessly. Also, I had my pride. Lynda touched my cheek. We listened to late night jazz the rest of the way home.

Sunday night I got the usual butterflies. I've been told a lot of people do. Probably a holdover from school days.

The phone interrupted my thoughts. "Hello," I answered.

"Matt, how are you?" said the caller.

"Good to hear your voice, George. I'm trying to get a handle on things." I responded.

"What have you been doing? The last time we talked you had set up an appointment with your accountant."

"Yes, Lynda and I had dinner with some of her friends Saturday night. Today, I've been trying to relax, like you suggested — reading the paper, taking it slow, and thinking."

"Glad to year you're relaxing. What have you been thinking about?"

"Oh, mostly that I've been depressed — that I won't be going into Technology, Inc., tomorrow, that I don't have a job. I've got my usual Sunday night butterflies. On top of that, I'm out of work and I don't really know what to do." George just listened. I continued, "Also, Lynda and I had a discussion about vacation. We may not be able to go out to the West Coast. I'm worried about money."

"You're dealing with a lot. Take things one step at a time. Tomorrow you'll be seeing your accountant. Hopefully, he'll be able to help you sort some things out. And remember, you can call me anytime."

"Thanks, George. It helps to be reminded. How about a run tomorrow?"

"I'm seeing clients early in the morning. How about late in the afternoon?"

"Great. See you at the beginning of the path about 4:30."

Even with my good friend George, it took effort, you might call it courage, to get past my vulnerability. Don't get me wrong. Others I knew had had to search high and low for support. I had people offering to help. I wrestled with accepting it. To do so, I had to expose my hurt, my feelings. I was used to having a good time with friends and relating to colleagues on a professional, not such a personal, level.

On Monday, Lynda and I arrived at Russ's office just before two o'clock. His secretary directed us to take a seat at the conference table, assuring us that he'd be along shortly.

Russ was about thirty-eight years old. If there was one word that described Russ it was *responsible.* The art collaborative that Linda works with uses Russ as their accountant.

Surveying the office, I was reminded of Russ's hobbies — restoring old cars and collecting sports memorabilia. His office looked like a sports writer's den. There were yellowed baseball newspaper clippings framed and hanging on the walls, a Louisville slugger leaning against the bookcase, a gold cup trophy inscribed "1972 Collegiate Champions" on the right-hand corner of his desk, and a putter resting against the window sill.

As Russ walked in he said, "Don't get up. Good to see you. Just give me a moment to get settled."

As we began to talk, I had a hard time accepting that I'd have to cut my health club membership, one of my biggest pleasures. We also decided to trade in our one-year-old Buick and lease a smaller car. There was a big difference between $350 car payments and a $220 lease.

Russ was not one to mince words or waste time. He began, "Remember these times are temporary. We'll develop a flexible plan that can be adjusted as your situation changes."

"A plan," Lynda asked.

"Yes, a budget."

Lynda replied, "That's reassuring, Russ. What do you think we ought to base our budget on?"

"This doesn't have to be complicated," Russ said. "From what you've told me, we'll consider five primary factors. They are your combined incomes, including Matt's severance and your savings.

We'll also consider Chris's next semester's tuition and your necessary monthly expenses. The fifth factor is the one that is least predictable — the amount of time it will take you to get a job. These days it could take a year or more. In your case, I'm assuming that you'll be looking for a professional full-time position in your related field."

Chris was our son, a senior at the Business School. He lived in an apartment near the campus and had applied to M.B.A. programs for the coming year.

"Russ," I exclaimed. "It's hard for me to imagine that I could be out of work for a year!"

Calmly, Russ responded, "I based my one-year estimate on current statistics, plus I added a couple of months as a cushion. After we agree on a time line, then we can define a realistic plan. My goal is to help you and Lynda minimize your financial concerns."

I responded, "Makes sense." And I thought, The last time I *had* to look for a job was after I graduated from college. It's a lot more complex now.

"Matt, Russ is trying to plan conservatively so that you can put your energy into job searching instead of worrying about money. I know we'll still have our concerns, but we'll also have a plan to guide us."

"Okay, Okay, I understand."

"I don't want to misrepresent things," Russ added. "As Lynda said, you'll still have financial concerns. I've worked with others who have lost their jobs or decided to change careers. You're making a big change. Struggle is part of it, but planning helps. Believe me, you'll both be fine."

I was nodding. Then Lynda said, "Let's discuss our vacation."

"What about it?" Russ asked.

"Well," I quickly interjected, "I don't think we can afford to go to the West Coast this summer as we planned. When Lynda and I initially talked about it, I was working."

Lynda protested. "Matt, I haven't seen my family in over a year."

"What do you expect me to say at this point? I'm out of work!"

"Wait, how about postponing your vacation until the fall?" asked Russ. He continued, "That's seven or eight months from now. You could have a job by September or October."

No one spoke for about ten seconds. Then I broke the silence. "Lynda, what do you think?"

"Ah, mmm, that sounds reasonable. Maybe I can get my brother to visit us this spring."

I put my hand on my stomach and thought, What a relief.

During our hour-and-a-half meeting we developed a weekly and monthly budget. We also agreed to check in with Russ if we thought we needed to change the budget.

Russ walked us to the door. As I shook his hand I said, "How long have you had that 'Back to Basics' poster hanging above the file?"

"Oh, quite a while. You know though, it's interesting, more people have commented on it in the past six months or so."

"Mmm. Hey Russ, keep practicing that golf swing!"

"Hey, my pleasure. Take care, Lynda . . . Matt."

On the way home I said, "Seeing Russ helped us talk over some important issues." Then I turned to Lynda and said, half kiddingly, "In a pinch, I could sell my favorite watch."

She shrugged her shoulders. "Oh, it wouldn't get you much now anyway!"

"Makes sense."

"Our goal is to avoid shooting from the hip. Instead we can get sound advice from Russ and others."

"And use good old common sense."

Back to Basics

Health

Family

Education

Friendship

Recreation

Financial Planning

Tuesday morning came, a work day, but not for me. I had no appointments and no work. I walked to the door, waving good-bye to Lynda. When she was out of sight, I sat down at the table gripping and staring at my coffee cup. As closely as I could tell, I was feeling embarrassed and lost. I didn't want anybody to see me sitting here; I was supposed to be at work. I wasn't sure what to do. George's "Try to relax" was well intended, but *I'd lost my job!* How could I relax?

Finally, when I checked the time, I realized that Lynda had been gone for nearly two hours. I had spaced out.

My briefcase was resting in its familiar corner, reminding me of our meeting with Russ and my job — my ex-job. I interrupted my paralysis by sorting through my briefcase, one pocket at a time. The last time it had been empty was when I carried it home from the store. Each pocket represented my office: a place for everything. I unpacked and examined its contents: a ruler, a red pen and number 2 pencil, a folder labeled "To Do @ Home" containing an article titled "Managing Tomorrow's Organization Today," a blank yellow pad, staff meeting notes, a project proposal draft, and my Rolodex file on disk. This Rolodex disk — vendor contacts, associates from past jobs, and colleagues from Technology, Inc. — would become invaluable.

During the afternoon, I talked myself into doing some of the grocery shopping. One of my biggest concerns was who would see me; I was supposed to be at work. I contemplated wearing a coat and tie. Then if I ran into someone, at least I could say I was en route from work, buying some things for a late lunch at home.

That evening I felt lonely, but I didn't want to be alone, not completely. Inside, I had an unsettled, anxious, irritated feeling. Yes, I had a severance, a financial plan, good friends, and a supportive wife, but *I had lost my job.* I thought, I'm not sure Lynda would understand my mood. I didn't feel like talking, so I put on my coat and took a walk. I just walked; the cold air kept me moving.

As I look back to my first full week of job loss, Tuesday, Wednesday, and Thursday felt like a wash. The only thing that saved Friday and, quite frankly, gave me some faith was an article,

"Post Job Loss Trauma," I read in our local newspaper. It confirmed many of my feelings and my mood. I wasn't odd or crazy. It said that many people who lose their jobs feel victimized, isolated, self-doubting, and occasionally paralyzed. It also gave advice to those who have lost their jobs, basically:

1. Don't isolate yourself for extended periods of time. Associate and talk with others.
2. Stay active in ways that make you feel good. (In my case, I'd contine to run and would take walks.)
3. Develop a schedule. For example, have breakfast as you would if you were going to your past job, build in an exercise routine, and schedule time to visit someone—a friend, colleague, past associate. Spend part of your time out of the house.

The weekend was easier. Everyone had it off. I didn't have to worry about explaining to anyone.

After a week or so, the reality of the layoff began to sink in for both Lynda and me. Bless her, she was such a pillar of strength when I first came home with the news. She was still supportive most of the time, but now she was beginning to feel angry. Many of our social contacts were connected with my past employer, and she missed our routine of leaving at the same time in the morning, kissing, and wishing each other a good day—not to mention the financial security. She felt helpless, watching me wrestle with my feelings and the unknown.

Sometimes Lynda would say, "I'm scared. It's not fair!" I'd have my own fears and would get annoyed, thinking I was the only one who was entitled to those feelings. In fact, I discovered, my wife was clearer about her feelings than I was about mine.

At that point, the only thing I had done specifically to look for a job was to call Jesse, one of my former colleagues. Jesse was a newly promoted vice president of manufacturing at Integrate, Inc., a growing software company. I had heard through the grapevine that Jesse had two openings for management staff: one for national and the other for international operations. I figured it wouldn't hurt to call. He was bound to consider me before he would a stranger.

His number was readily available on my Rolodex disk. After hours he was likely to pick up his own phone, so I rang him at about 5:15. Jesse answered, "Matt Townden, I haven't heard from you in a while. How're you?"

"Well, that's what I'm calling about. I could be better." I paused and there was a silence, so I continued. "Technology, Inc., let me go last week. They're cutting back in manufacturing; said there were too many managers in the division, so they laid me off." God, I thought as I spoke those words, Jesse just got promoted and I got laid off.

"Sorry to hear that, Matt. What can I do for you?"

I took a deep breath and said, "That's why I'm calling. I heard that you were promoted. Congratulations. Uh . . . Also, I was told that you have two managerial openings."

There was another pause. Finally, Jesse said, "Well, we're being very selective in our hiring process. I've hand picked a hiring team of five others who are screening resumés as a first step. You know, there's a lot of competition these days. We've got to make the absolute right hire."

This was not what I'd expected. Jesse continued, "Matt, you're welcome to send me your resumé. I'll put it on the top of the pile."

"Pile?" I echoed.

"Yes. Within the past two weeks, we've reviewed more than three hundred resumés."

I blurted out, "That's discouraging."

Jesse quipped, "That's the market!"

"Okay Jesse, I'm glad you're doing well. I'll rewrite my resumé to include Technology, Inc., and send it along." I couldn't wait to get off the phone. "Thanks for your time." After I hung up, I wheeled around and kicked the wastebasket.

I was offended by Jesse's lumping me into the same pile as all those other applicants. Rather than dealing with his objections, I took them personally. I'd almost hung up on him. Later on in my transition, I learned that I'd allowed myself to become part of the pile. As I became more clear about my skills and talents, as well as what I wanted, I learned to overcome objections. The bottom line is that everyone — even those you know best — needs to be convinced that you are the best choice.

One night we invited George over for dinner. I read part of the article "Post Job Loss Trauma" to George and Lynda, hoping to get their reactions. I began, "At work most of us got rewarded for our expertise, performance, productivity, and political savvy. We didn't get rewarded for our feelings. In fact, many of us have learned to be judicious about expressing our feelings. The effects could be pigeon-holing, loss of power, and possible dismissal."

They listened attentively. I continued, "It seems that part of what we got paid for was *not* to feel. Consequently, many who lose their jobs don't know what to feel — about their work, about their past employer, or about being laid off."

"Excuse me," Lynda said, "What's the plus side of knowing your feelings?"

"Good question," answered George. "If people become more conscious of what they feel, they can become more competent at managing their emotions. They can use that energy to help them define and stretch toward new goals."

"George, it says here, 'If we can identify and name our feelings, then there's a higher probability we can channel our feelings into positive action.'" As I read this, I flashed on my conversation with Jesse at Integrate, Inc.

Lynda commented, "It sounds like it doesn't make sense to interview for a job until you've sorted out your feelings."

George nodded.

"I guess what you and the article are saying makes sense. I don't necessarily want to hear it; it means more work and, I would guess, pain."

"Matt," Lynda replied, "You've already had the experience of looking for a job before sorting through your feelings and confusion. That's like placing the cart before the horse."

"Besides," she continued, "You might end up where you don't want to be. I imagine that would be a lot more painful."

"Yes, Lynda. Matt, remember the conversation we had the day after you were let go. I agree with Lynda, you've got to talk about your feelings and sort out some of your options before you start interviewing."

"George, can you tell us about some of your clients who learned to manage their feelings?" asked Lynda.

"Recently, I worked with an advertising manager who lost her job during a downsizing. She felt angry and had been discriminated against. We worked together for eight sessions, during which she gained confidence and sorted out her feelings, skills, and values. She vowed she'd land on her feet. As she talked about her priorities and networked, she looked for a boss who respected her and for a company with a vision and products that she felt contributed to the world. Through learning from every situation and trusting her feelings, she achieved her goal."

"How long did it take?"

"She was unusual. She made her transition a full-time effort and landed a job in five months. Fundamentally, talking helped my client get things off her chest and develop other strategies. She found ways of dealing with her frustrations and became more focused."

The article proved to be a catalyst for quite a conversation. I tossed and turned all night, sensing that I was getting ready to embark on a new journey. I knew that I was scared, but somehow I was also feeling excited. Scared, mostly because I was used to being in control. I had been paid for having the answers. I had been in charge of taking care of individuals and company problems. Now I was facing my own. The exciting part was the opportunity to learn about myself and to figure out where I would work next.

After three weeks in my jobless journey, I discovered that learning never goes to waste. I remembered that in a corporate career management class, the trainer drew a simple line graph. He labeled the vertical axis "Control" and the horizontal axis "Uncertainty." "After a job loss," he had explained, "when control diminishes, uncertainty increases." This must be, at least in part, the reason I was feeling so much stress. I was the one people had come to for advice and help. Now the shoe was on the other foot. Now, I began to think, *I* needed support and professional guidance.

I got into a daily habit of looking at the help wanted ads. The classifieds were sparse, compared to a couple of years ago, and I didn't know what I was looking for. This only depressed me more.

Lynda would say, "At least 75 percent of the people I know found their jobs through networking. Haven't you heard of the hidden job market!?"

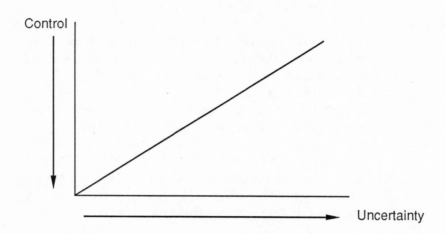

I'd say, "I'm being lazy. I just thought I might get lucky flipping through the paper."

We took turns every other night: when I cooked dinner, Lynda would do the dishes, and vice versa. When Lynda cooked, I'd sit at the dining room table, flipping through the help wanted pages. Lynda would just about shout, "The only thing you'll get from the paper is ink on your finger tips!"

Unfortunately, even at my management level, my severance package did not include outplacement services. At the time, four months' pay with full benefits seemed like a reasonable offer. As I drove to Dr. Robinez's office for my yearly physical, I thought about the process of getting career guidance. I used to feel guilty taking time off from work to go to the doctor's. Those guilty feelings were haunting me again.

"Dr. Robinez, what do you think?"

"Matt, your healthy diet and daily runs must be paying off."

"Good news."

"But you do look worried today."

I hesitated for a moment, and I'm sure I looked surprised. Dr. Robinez had a soothing aura that said Trust me. I caught my breath and said, "I was laid off about two weeks ago . . . lost my job."

Dr. Robinez was about sixty. She was from Spain and had a

comforting face and her eyes emanated wisdom. She said, "Tell me your story. I have time. What happened?"

As I talked, I felt the worry, lined in my forehead, begin to disappear. My shoulders relaxed as she listened. She just *listened.*

That evening after dinner I said to Lynda, "Dr. Robinez encouraged me to talk about being laid off. She called it 'telling my story.' It wasn't until the end of my exam that I opened up."

"That sounds helpful. What made you talk with her?"

"I was avoiding conversation at the beginning of the exam, probably because she's usually so busy and because I wanted to protect myself from any kind of judgment. Then, in her sincere manner, she asked me what happened."

"Matt, you looked relieved. Maybe you should consider finding someone to talk with on a regular basis."

"How about you?"

"I can't be . . ."

"You're my wife."

"I can't be the only one you talk with. Honey, you need someone more objective."

"What are you saying?"

"Like you, I need a break from all this stuff sometimes. I'd like us to talk about other things besides layoff, jobs, and money."

"I feel like a dog with his tail between his legs. Does this mean you don't want to listen?"

"No, not at all. Please don't misunderstand me. I care very much about you and your career. I just can't give you all the help you need. I think a fresh perspective is necessary—like when we were in couples therapy. That's all."

I thought for a moment about how I had resisted couples therapy and about that old cliché: it's one thing to think about getting help and another to do something about it.

"I think I understand. I'll talk it over with George."

"That's a good idea, talk with George. Also, why don't you ask George about a support group? I have a friend who can't say enough about the guidance she got from her group."

"One thing at a time. But I'll try to talk about other things, too. With you, I mean. I know this situation can get wearing."

Asking George to be my counselor was out of the question.

Don't Panic

Do's and Don'ts

DO . . .

- Focus on one or two practical things you can do to support you and your family (for example, develop a budget).

- Take things one step at a time.

- Ask for advice; check with others.

- Plan conservatively. In a slow economy it will take more time to find work.

- Develop a schedule, one you can change when you need to.

- Talk about your feelings.

- Consider seeking professional help.

DON'T . . .

- Try to look for all the answers and/or solve them at once.

- Project far into the future (for instance, worrying about what will happen if your severance runs out).

- Sell your belongings or make a drastic change based on fear.

- Let you or anyone else label you odd or crazy.

- Start interviewing.

- Think there is only one way to solve your problems.

I believe that mixing friendship and a professional relationship rarely works. Furthermore, as much as I trusted George, I wanted objective professional guidance from someone who did not know me.

I needed to talk about my feelings, begin to articulate some of my future goals, and stay honest with myself. I wanted a career counselor to help guide me toward meaningful work.

3

Story Telling

Healing talk

George referred me to three career counselors. After twenty-minute phone interviews with each, I chose to work with John. He listened well and had a direct approach and an upbeat manner. In addition to a master's degree in counseling, John had experience as a social worker, corporate recruiter, and had spent five years as an independent career consultant.

"Matt," John explained, "I won't waste your time. With my guidance you'll be able to get on with your life by clarifying your needs and materializing your goals."

"John, I like what you have to say. When can we meet? I've been out of work for about three weeks, and I'm getting anxious about getting on with things."

"Will tomorrow at eleven suit you?"

"Sure. I didn't expect that I'd be able to come in so soon. I'll see you tomorrow."

Arranging the meeting with John had the same calming effect as setting up our visit with Russ. Support seemed to be an essential part of this process.

Russ's advice to curtail large expenses and to think twice before eating in expensive restaurants was working. Once a week we treated ourselves to Chinese food at Lucky Garden or a pizza at Angelo's. I felt like I was dating my wife again!

During breakfast Lynda said, "I'm proud of you for setting up the meeting with John. How do you feel about seeing him?"

"Thanks, sweetie. I'm looking forward to it. I'm a little apprehensive, but for the most part I'm feeling it's time to get on with things."

Leaving myself time for a cup of coffee at the deli in town, I arrived at John's office just before eleven. His office was located opposite the town common in his home, an old Victorian that had been converted into condominiums.

I climbed the stairs, appreciating the workmanship of the carved banister. At the top of the stairs was an open area, brightened by a skylight. I sat in the chair next to a potted plant. As I leaned back, I noticed the skylight was an old-fashioned hexagonal shape.

My head turned as the door to my right opened. Suddenly an angora cat scurried across the Oriental rug and down the stairs. "That's Cabot. I'm John," said the soft-spoken man. He continued, "You must be Matt. Please come in."

We both looked at each other for a moment, then I said, "Good to meet you. What seat would you like me to take?" For some reason I was anxious to sit down.

John smiled and replied, "Your choice."

I took the chair opposite the window that overlooked the town common.

John began, "I understand from our conversation yesterday that you've lost your job. You mentioned it's been about three weeks."

"That's so. I got laid off."

"By the way," John said, "don't worry about the time, I'll let you know when the time is about up. Our first session will be an hour and a half. Unless we agree otherwise, the following sessions are an hour in length. I extend the first session because there's usually a lot of ground to cover, what with getting to know you and all."

"Sounds good to me."

"I'm going to encourage you to talk about how you felt being laid off. I want to assure you that the feelings you have are normal, that they will pass, and that you can depend on me for guidance."

I nodded and said, "I think I do need to talk." I paused for a moment; John relaxed, with his legs crossed.

In an encouraging voice he said, "Matt, it's not easy for anyone to begin."

I looked up and said, "I'm not sure where to start. When . . ."

"Yes," John prompted, "when you were laid off . . ."

"I felt dehumanized, like I was a number, not a person. I felt like one of the bodies sacrificed up to the 'We have to make a profit' gods. That company was an S.O.B.!" John nodded slightly. "Mr. Carroll was worse than an S.O.B."

"Mr. Carroll?"

"Yes, my boss. Everyone referred to him as 'Mr. Control.' You know. A starched-shirt fast tracker."

"Got it. You sound pretty angry with him."

"You know, he just didn't care how I worked or how hard I worked. *How* I achieved results didn't matter. All he cared about was the numbers. This whole thing isn't fair."

"This whole thing?"

"Yeah, getting the boot."

I looked down for a moment, caught my breath, and said, "This is a tough one to share. I had a dream a few nights before our meeting. I dreamt I was homeless. I was pushing a grocery cart with nowhere to go."

"Mmm, that *is* a tough one." He paused for a moment and then added, "You have every right to feel angry and rejected. Venting with me is appropriate—but remember, not with a potential employer."

"I think I know what you mean. That's why I'm here, right? To vent and clarify things with you."

"Yes, Matt. You also sound lonely and afraid. This makes a lot of sense, given that you've left behind what was familiar. You're facing many unknowns and you're in pain."

"What do I do?"

"Good question. First, I want to reassure you again that these feelings are normal and they will pass."

"I have my doubts."

"Of course you do . . . you've just had a tremendous loss. Healing and a positive outlook will take time. Matt, for now, I'm going to give you an assignment."

"An assignment?"

"Yes, this is it. I want you to do some story telling. Talk with people that will listen and not judge — as you've done with me."

I recalled my conversation with Dr. Robinez: she also had encouraged me to tell my story.

John explained, "Talk with different people about your loss so that you can connect with what you're really feeling. Imagine you're replaying a film. Recall that this happened, then this happened, then that happened."

"What good will that do?"

"First, by telling your story, you have the opportunity to share your feelings and to name them. Second, you can filter out what you do and don't want to share with a potential employer."

"Okay, I'll try telling my story."

"Matt, let's talk a bit about beliefs. Over the past couple of years, I've met several people who have lost their jobs. Many continue to believe that their employer should have taken care of them or that their boss knew what was best for them. These beliefs too often get in the way of people's career mobility."

"I guess, but that's the way it seemed to me, too: If I did my job and didn't ruffle too many feathers, my job would be safe. At least, until *I* decided to leave."

"Believe me, I can see how you and so many others learned to think that way. My point is that these beliefs are no longer constructive. Today, no one's job is secure, and everyone must be taking responsibility for his or her own career."

"Have I ever been hearing that one!"

"For example, Matt, I'm suggesting that you and so many others are not to blame for being laid off. Blaming yourself and, for that matter, people like Mr. Carroll is limiting. Your layoff was circumstantial, not personal, although I know at this point it *feels* personal, and for now Mr. Carroll would be the most likely to blame."

"You know it's hard to admit, but I think you're right. It was business; the company needed to save money. I was caught in the shuffle. But I still think Mr. Carroll was an S.O.B."

"To different degrees, I expect that you'll be venting your feelings for some time. Your job, colleagues, and company meant a lot to you. I simply don't want you to believe that something is true when it is not. Eventually, such beliefs could get in the way of your job search process. Let me tell you a story about someone whose beliefs got in the way."

"Mmm . . . good idea."

"First, I'd like to remind you that another benefit of telling *your* story will be to clarify your beliefs. Your clarity will lead you to drop beliefs that no longer work, keep the ones that do, and learn new ones that support your mobility."

John paused for a moment then said, "Now, the story. Recently I worked with a top-notch salesperson who was fired. Her boss thought she was dipping into the till, so to speak. Soon thereafter, she began to believe that she was a lousy salesperson. Her confidence began to seriously wane, preventing her from interviewing competitively."

"What happened?"

"Well, during a three-session three-week time frame, she was able to see how she was perpetuating a myth. I asked her questions about her performance, sales figures, and her client relationships. We gathered some real data. In fact, she had won 'Salesperson of the Year' two years in a row. She also talked about the anger she had toward a boss whom she had regarded as her mentor."

"Did she also feel ashamed?"

"Oh yes, that too. As she talked about her feelings and her experiences, she began to let go of that crippling myth."

"Did she finally get a job?"

"Well, the last time we talked was around two weeks ago. She reported feeling more confident and that she was a finalist for a challenging sales position. Regarding her relationship with her ex-boss, that will take some time to heal. On the other hand, she is clear enough to talk positively about her successful past experience with her former employer."

"Thanks, that was a good example."

"Much of what we've been talking about boils down to what I call a career lattice approach."

Benefits of Story Telling

- You'll share and name your feelings.

- You'll develop a clear "no sour grapes" explanation as to why you lost your job.

- You'll uncover your skills.

- You'll gain focus on what to do next.

- You'll get feedback.

- You'll filter out what you do and don't want to say to an employer.

- You'll drop those beliefs that no longer work, keep the ones that do, and learn new ones that support your career mobility.

"Career *lattice?*"

John explained, "Many professionals during the eighties were on a vertical fast track within organizations that were growing and saw no apparent end in sight. Like barnacles, professionals clung to the rungs — supervisors, managers, directors, vice presidents — and progressed upward as the ship moved forward. This is no longer the case. For the most part, the career ladder is defunct. Now, with downsizing and restructuring as the norm, organizations can no longer support thousands of career ladders."

"Like at Technology, Inc."

"Yes. These same professionals must look at another way of creating their careers. I call this the 'career lattice approach.' Just for a moment visualize a lattice."

"You mean like a criss-crossed fence that ivy grows along?"

"Exactly. You must have a garden."

"We do."

"How does the ivy grow?"

"I guess in any direction it pleases," I chuckled. "Often into places where we don't want it."

John nodded. "The ivy grows up or down and to either side. For you and the majority of job seekers, to have success in this changed market you've got to grow like the ivy using a lattice for support."

"How do you mean?"

"I'll leave you with this. In our future sessions I'm going to encourage you to think and act in terms of your skills, values, and interests. Then, I'll suggest that you develop and try different paths that will match your skills, values, and interests with opportunities."

"But I'm a manager."

"Yes, you have been, although in this market, titles have less meaning. It's what you can do and how you do it that count. Once you find yourself another position, then you can negotiate for a title. You've got to know what you want and how you can add value to an organization or your customers, and then you have to stay flexible, like the ivy."

"Mmm, I guess. But, just one more thing. Stay flexible — what exactly do you mean?"

"I think that job seekers need to learn not to ask for permission to do what they want. Instead, I believe they need to take responsibility. One way is to ask for feedback. Asking permission is putting your destiny into the hands of others. On the other hand, taking and asking for feedback stretches you toward possibilities. It's a means of discovering and learning how to do what you want to do."

"So when you talk about flexibility you mean being open to learning but not looking to others to make your decisions."

"That's what I mean. We'll talk more next week. Remember, tell your story."

On the way home I felt more alive than I had felt in the past several months, including while I was employed! I realized that it was necessary that I express the anger that had built up toward Mr. Carroll, Technology, Inc., and getting the boot. When I was in counseling with Lynda, I recalled feeling better after talking about things. The same was true with my job-related issues. If I didn't express my anger, I'd be exploding about what seemed to be the little things, like I did when Lynda forgot to pick up

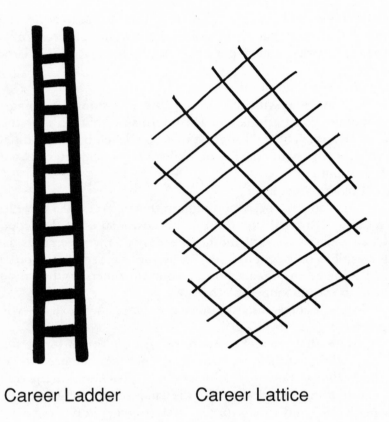

Career Ladder   Career Lattice

my shirts from the cleaners. Walking into the house, I glanced at the slogan on John's card:

A ladder no longer, but a lattice that works.

Already, I was thinking about other questions and sorting through possible answers. During a career seminar at Technology, Inc., the trainer had used a metaphor I could apply not only to the telling of my own story but also to future networking. The concept was that we are all running a businees called "Life, Inc." You are the chairperson of the board of directors for Life, Inc. (your life). It's your primary job to run the company (your life) in the black. Part of your obligation is to select board members who support, challenge, and guide you toward your goals. Board members can be animate—such as friends, colleagues, a pet, your spouse—or they can be inanimate—such as a journal, a special place you go to think, or a symbol that gives you strength. Already my board members included Lynda, George, Russ, and John. Two other potential members I planned to approach were professional colleagues: Maria, a human resource manager, and Eric, a management consultant. They had always been good listeners in the past.

So far it felt relatively safe, but not easy, to ask for support from family and friends. It's never been a simple matter when it comes to asking for help, at least not for me. Part of my reluctance was a matter of pride, and part stemmed from my hurt. Often I felt torn between isolation and associating with others.

I was getting into the habit of skimming two newspapers a day, the local one and the *Wall Street Journal.* They provided some ideas and were a good source for timely articles. For example, one article reminded me about the necessity of stretching beyond the familiar. Eventually, I would need to network with "strangers"— not something I relished. When the time came, my "board" would most likely be supportive in this effort.

During the next week, I practiced telling my story. It seemed

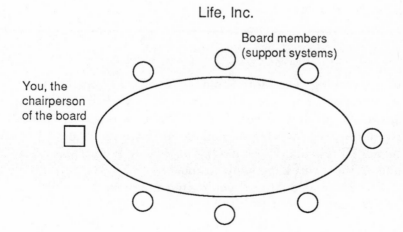

Life, Inc.

Board members (support systems)

You, the chairperson of the board

Story Telling

Do's and Don'ts

DO . . .

- Interview two or three counselors before you make a decision.
- Practice telling your story; talk about and clarify what happened.
- Ask for and accept feedback.
- Examine your beliefs.
- Consider different paths to achieve your goals.
- Begin selecting a support team.

DON'T . . .

- Bad mouth your past employer to colleagues or anyone that might become a potential employer.
- Ask permission to think about different ideas or to try new things.
- Rely exclusively on the traditional career ladder.
- Reject support.

---

to be working. The more I told it, the better I began to understand myself. For example, when I talked with Eric, my management consultant friend, I said, "When I was let go, I felt like twenty years of work was yanked out from under me." I continued, "I felt like I was having an out-of-body experience—like, Why is this happening to me?"

Eric responded, "Matt, you're in a tough situation. I'm glad you're talking about it. Have you been talking with Lynda?"

"I've been holding back some because I don't want to worry her and sound like 'poor me.'"

"You mean you don't want her to see you as weak?"

"Yeah," I muttered.

"Matt, I've learned that 'poor me' is human and temporary. Also, Lynda believes in you. I'd talk with her about your other concerns."

My anger and resentment toward the company and Mr. Carroll gradually began to diminish. I didn't feel the hurt as intensely. Less focus on them left me more energy for my self-discovery and job search. But I did know colleagues who were very productive in their current jobs but still carried pain and resentment for years after being laid off, so it was important to really vent these issues now. There were people on my team (Life, Inc.) I could connect with regarding a specific need and others like Lynda and George who also could be comforting.

During the week I basically forgot about looking for a job. No more help wanted ads for now! I concentrated on talking with people like George, Mike Fielder, my buddy at Technology, Inc., and Eric, my management consultant friend. I talked with them about how it felt to be laid off and about some of my aspirations. I must have said to all of them, "This time around, one of my top priorities will be to find a job that feels like a natural fit."

4

Step by Step

One at a time, you'll learn new skills

It was Thursday again, time to meet with John for the second time. I'm a morning person, so we scheduled for ten o'clock. As I waited in the reception area, I realized I was feeling anxious but a little less reticent.

"John!" I exclaimed, "I'm feeling a little better. I told my story to six of my friends and colleagues. I don't feel 100 percent, but I do think I can look at some of the practical aspects of my job search."

John nodded in his accepting manner and then responded, "You sound better—and it's important that you continue telling your story. As you do, I recommend that you keep a journal. Your journal could be viewed as analogous to a good friend. It's a place to express and clarify your thoughts, observations, feelings, and goals."

"I see. Will this journal take the place of talking with others?"

"Not at all, but it will be an additional asset."

"Okay, I'll think about it. John, I'm feeling a lot of uncertainty about the future, but I feel that some resolution is taking place. It's been five weeks. Now what I'm most concerned about is where I'm going."

"Much of this process has to do with trusting. Out of your day-to-day self-discovery and marketplace research, you'll find your direction. You'll learn to trust that your primary focus will come into view. For now, I'd like you to continue talking with others and consider starting a journal."

"This is tough for me. I've been getting paid for getting things done. You know, results."

"You'll still get results, but you'll become more aware of yourself and others along the way. Remember what I said . . ."

Before John could finish his sentence, I said, "In our first meeting you mentioned I'd be able to name my feelings and be better able to sell myself to a potential employer."

"Yes sir! That's what I said, and these are your goals, for now." He paused. "Matt, during this session I'd like to talk with you about competencies."

"Competencies?"

"Yes, competencies, or your skills. Knowing your competencies is an essential part of the lattice approach we talked about in our first session — creating different paths to get more meaningful work. A competency is a skill that can enable someone to perform in an outstanding manner, in your case for the purpose of getting a job. Although they can be interconnected, in other sessions we can talk about your professional competencies — the ones specifically related to your job."

"What are some examples of my job-getting competencies?"

"Well, skills like networking and interviewing and also questioning, problem solving, planning, and negotiating."

"Mmm. I see. A job-getting skill like problem solving could also be one of my professional skills."

"Right."

"John, I'm beginning to get the picture. You're talking about two skill sets: one, the skills necessary to get a job, and the other, the skills required to perform professionally. We are concentrating on the first."

"Yes, as you learn to hone these skills, name and manage your feelings, develop flexible plans, and network creatively, your goal will come into focus."

"Sometimes it's hard to believe that I can manage all of this."

"Things can get overwhelming."

"That's often how I feel."

John thought for a moment and responded, "Take things step by step, one at a time. When you're feeling confused or pressured, pause and sit back, take a deep breath, pause again, then ask yourself, 'What is one thing, just one thing I can do to get unstuck?' Trusting yourself and sticking with the process of developing your job-getting skills are key. This won't be easy, but you'll learn how."

I noted it down:

Take things step by step; pause or sit back, take a deep breath, pause again, then ask myself "What is one thing, just one thing I can do to get unstuck?"

"John, one of my biggest challenges will be patience. Hopefully, with your guidance, my sense is that I'll be able to manage these tough times and progress toward finding meaningful work."

"That's right, Matt. In our last ten minutes or so, I'd like to talk about what I call the 'inner work' and the 'outer work.' The inner work represents those issues that require more internal examination as you learn to negotiate your transition. For example, some of these issues are support, attitude, and values."

John paused and I said, "Those spring flowers over on the table are one of nature's symbols of hope. Even though it's a drizzly, cloudy day, I'm seeing what is positive."

"Flowers are a bright spot," agreed John. "Matt, I know it can be difficult to focus, but I want you to stay with me right now." He paused and looked at me seriously for a moment, then continued. "The outer work refers to those concerns that are more external to your search process."

"Do you mean issues like finances and job interviewing?"

"You've got it. And another would be selling yourself."

"John, I know it's about time to end. I just wanted to say that you've helped me realize that I've done some of the inner and outer work already. You're helping me wake up. I was paid for my planning and negotiating skills at Technology, Inc., not for my feelings. As I learn to express and manage my feelings, I can better use some of my . . . competencies."

"Good insights," John replied, then looked at the clock and

Inner Work *plus* Outer Work = WORK

Instructions: Complete the inner work and outer work lists with your own examples.

Inner Work

- Problem solving
- Decision making
- Listening
- Positive self-talk
- Evaluating experiences
- Clarifying values
- _____
- _____
- _____
- _____

Outer Work

- Planning
- Networking
- Interviewing
- Questioning
- Story telling
- Selling
- _____
- _____
- _____
- _____

Question: What inner work and/or outer work competencies will you focus on next? Choose two.

1.

2.

continued, "It's about eleven o'clock, but before we part I'd like to give you a couple of assignments." John sat forward. "The first is to pick a time each day for writing in your journal. I'd like you to write about your observations, about your feelings, and about people who you admire in the world."

"Such as Mother Teresa," I said.

John nodded and smiled.

As he handed me a worksheet he said, "For the second assignment as you think about your transition and job search process,

I'd like you to name some of the competencies that comprise the inner and outer work for getting a job. For instance, an inner-work competency is problem solving and . . ."

I finished John's sentence, "An outer-work competency is daily planning."

On the way home, my head was filled with converging thoughts. I needed to buy a journal. I should stop at the post office for stamps. It was time to dig out my old resumé. I wanted to call George this evening. I was excited and found myself wondering where I'd end up working. Tonight I was going to write about Mother Teresa. I stopped for the red flashing light at the five-way intersection about two miles from our house. My thoughts were like the cars, I realized, scrambling for a position and direction. I imagined myself in a helicopter hovering overhead; the cars would have looked like bumper cars at the carnival. But with patience, perseverance, and some skill, the drivers—and my thoughts—would reach their destinations. No doubt there would be many intersections on my journey. With practice I'd get better at prioritizing, solving problems, and negotiating through the obstacles.

I bought stamps and a journal. These seemingly minute accomplishments were stepping-stones toward my destination. They symbolized movement. As I pulled into the driveway at about noon, the sun began to shine. What a welcome sight! The grass glistened as the sun dried the water droplets on each blade. I couldn't resist. I kneeled down and skimmed my hand along the top of the grass blades. I felt the cooling water on my warm hands. I had been so inner focused and concerned about not working during the past month that I'd missed the coming of spring. April was about over. During this moment I relaxed. I felt fortunate for who I was and what I had.

Even before I got laid off, I ate lunch at home, on the average, two times a week. My diet had always been a healthy one. Plenty of vegetables, turkey and chicken sandwiches with mustard (no mayo!) was my standard bill of fare, along with a bowl of soup (I liked Progresso), and sometimes I treated myself to a home-made chocolate chip cookie. I looked forward to lunch; it was a time for a break. I usually listened to jazz and read a sports magazine like *Runner's World* while I ate.

My transition and job search began to remind me of my marathoning days. I had been successful competing in six-kilometer races and had decided it was time for a greater challenge — a marathon. Practice involved a step-by-step improvement process and a couple of half marathon races (thirteen miles) to build my confidence and endurance. I viewed each half marathon as a breakthrough event. Training required a transition period, adjusting to increased mileage, tedious stretching, and strengthening exercises. I was ready for my first marathon after six months of training, which involved sixty to eighty practice miles per week.

I began to see that in job searching, as in marathoning, there were fits and starts. Sometimes it was difficult to put on my track shoes at 5:30 on a cold winter morning or to run twenty miles alone when I couldn't find a running mate. These were the tests. If I passed, they solidified my commitment, kept my passion alive, and propelled me toward my goal.

The start of the marathon was not when the official's gun went off. Departing from my routine was the start. Similarly, when I pushed some of the pain of job loss aside, at least temporarily stopped marching to the schedule at Technology, Inc., and took control by making decisions, like deciding with whom I would talk and about what, this was the real start of my job searching.

Taking action was leading me to tell my story and to write about my thoughts and feelings. When I felt overwhelmed, adjusting my steps led me to clarify my goals and revise my plan. I was beginning to trust the process that would lead me to the finish.

I put down my *Runner's World* magazine and picked up my journal. As I started at the first blank page, the word *marathon* came to mind, and I wrote:

April 26th

I'M RUNNING THE MARATHON . . . It's easy to blend into the crowd or to be talked into becoming part of it. There were often as many as ten thousand runners, and there are tens of thousands of people who have lost their jobs. Sometimes I'd think, What's the point of running? Like now I think, What's the point of looking for a job? At other times, I'd hear people say it couldn't be so difficult to run a marathon if so many others do it. Similarly, I'd hear that there are so many others who are

Action Planning for Career Mobility

Instructions: State your short-term goal, then answer each of the questions pertaining to it.

Note: Each of your short-term goals are steps in a series that will lead to your long-term goal: meaningful work.

1. Goal _____

What do I need to do next? _____

How much time is needed? _____

What resources are needed? _____

_____

2. Goal _____

What do I need to do next? _____

How much time is needed? _____

What resources are needed? _____

_____

3. Goal _____

What do I need to do next? _____

How much time is needed? _____

What resources are needed? _____

_____

laid off, it can't be that hard to find a job. Employers will understand; they'll give you a break!

In both situations, it's true; there are thousands out there, but experience has taught me that it's still difficult and painful. That's my challenge. The point is, it's my own race no matter how many are running. I have respect for every runner or every person who has lost a job—each of us *must go the distance. When I get discouraged in my job search, I'll think about running the marathon. I made it in that race. I'll make it in this one.*

Marathoning became a metaphor that helped guide me through my transition period. Marathoning, like job change, had a beginning, a middle, and an end. There were times of joy as well as obstacles and pain. My running history included five marathons, and each one took both "inner" and "outer" resources. On the inside I'd think, You can do it. On the outside I'd plant one foot after another, adjusting my speed accordingly.

Lynda came home at about eight that evening. "Honey," she announced, "I found the perfect present for Chris—a brass desk lamp. You know he's turning twenty-one this coming weekend."

I looked up from my journal and retorted, "I know he'll be twenty-one. He's my son too."

"What are *you* so irritated about?"

Your Personal Journal

Date:

_____

_____

_____

_____

_____

_____

_____

_____

_____

Awakenings

"What did the lamp cost?"

Lynda scowled. "It was my money. Thirty-five dollars. No big deal. I waited until it was on sale. You're just mad because you're out of work."

"You don't know what you're talking about."

"Matt, look in the mirror."

"You just don't understand."

"Understand what? You're out of work and Chris will only be twenty-one once. A nice desk lamp is the least we can do for him. I'm not shutting down everything for you. We can still afford a lamp."

I pouted for a while, then followed Lynda into the living room. She sat on one side of the sofa, and I took the wingback chair. She opened the newspaper. Within five minutes she looked up and asked, "What were you writing when I walked in?"

"I was writing in my journal."

"Something John recommended?" I was silent. She continued, "You never find time to write to Chris or our relatives on the West Coast."

We were reacting enough to each other, so I simply said, "This layoff situation is new for both of us. We are both trying to adjust." She leaned back and thought for a moment. I tried to relax with the silence as John did with me.

After what seemed to be a minute or two she sat forward. "Matt," she said, "I think that sometimes I get jealous about the time you spend learning about yourself. I also get intimidated. You seem to be growing so much."

I leaned forward, looking directly at Lynda, and said, "If you're concerned about us growing apart, forget it. We're a team."

As we both smiled, she added, "I'm relieved. Sometimes I overreact. Sorry."

"And sometimes I get scared." I paused. "May I see the lamp you bought Chris?"

Lynda smiled, "It's a banker's lamp. He'll like it. By the way, I wanted to mention that the principal at school posted an announcement for a public workshop titled 'Innovative Strategies for Career Mobility.' It's going to be held next Thursday evening at the community college auditorium." She reached into her briefcase. "Here's the flier. It looks interesting."

"I'll look it over."

Just before I turned out the light I read, "This is a highly pragmatic and motivational workshop where job seekers, career changers, including those laid off, will learn to focus, expand options, and get a great job." I kissed Lynda goodnight.

The next morning I called the career resource center to talk with the director of career programs. She explained that the objective of the program would be to introduce the notion and clarify the benefits of a skills- and values-driven job search based on self and marketplace research. Also, the presenter would demystify

---

Step by Step
Do's and Don'ts

DO . . .

- Practice telling your story.

- Start a journal. Write about your experiences and feelings.

- Distinguish between your professional skills and job-getting competencies.

- Practice patience. Allow for learning.

- Try again, step by step.

- Talk over financial concerns with your spouse, as painful as this might be.

- Allow for others' feelings; they're adjusting too.

DON'T . . .

- Belittle trying.

- Think you're unskilled.

- Take giant leaps.

- Bury what's bothering you.

- Walk away when others need to vent.

---

some of the myths about the marketplace and help everyone begin implementing a job search using this strategy. I signed up. It felt good that Lynda was watching out for me and that I was taking action. Step by step, I seemed to be moving toward my goal, and I wasn't even sure what it was . . . yet!

Attending workshops and meetings gave me events to look forward to and the chance to learn from and share with others. I was doing exactly what I had recommended others do when I was an employed senior manager. It was a different ball game to be a player when I was used to being the coach. I began to think that I'd be a lot better coach the next time around. I was getting first-hand experience about what it feels like to get laid off, get back on my feet, and get reemployed. Going through these rites of passage would be some of the best credentials I could bring to my next employer.

5

Passages

Your rites

On May 2, I wrote in my journal:

> *The phrase "a natural fit" keeps on coming to mind. I want to find a place and do work that feels like a natural fit. I admire people like Winston Churchill and Mother Teresa. They express themselves. They have been pioneers who have contributed to the world. They are expressing their inner beliefs outwardly. This is me. I'm questioning my fit in the corporate world. Maybe I need a different environment—a smaller company. Sometimes I feel my own friends don't recognize me. Or maybe I don't recognize them. That's okay; this process is about me, not them.*
>
> *Sometimes, expecially when I get anxious about being unemployed, I want to rush this process—get on the phone or walk through someone's door and ask for an interview. Simple as that! Then, I think of John's words, "Have faith, trust, you'll learn how."*
>
> *Writing helps me to sort things out.*

It was a sunny, seventy-degree day with a mild breeze. Perfect for painting the picket fence. The worn pickets were the ideal canvas for the white paint. The heat stretched the paint as my brush stroked each picket, and the streaks vanished almost instantly. I was enjoying working on a task that had a definite beginning and end.

My neighbor, Charlie, had retired as a senior vice president a couple of years ago. He had missed possibly two, maybe three days of work in his forty years' tenure with the same firm. As Charlie was strolling by, he stopped and said, "You must feel pretty lucky to be painting. I suppose you're thinking about finding a job."

"No," I responded, "I'm just painting." I was beginning to see that part of this process was learning to relax and be present. When I was meeting with John, I was meeting with John; when I was attending a seminar, I was attending a seminar; and when I was painting the picket fence, I was painting the picket fence.

"How ya doing, Matt?" said the mail carrier as he handed me a note from my son, Chris.

"Okay. Could be better. I'm getting there."

"We all are!"

Chris's note said,

Dad,
I can imagine these times can get tough, but you've got what it takes to get a great job.
                              Love,
                                Chris
P.S. Patience and perseverance.

I'd been giving Chris that same advice for years! Most important, my family members and friends listened and encouraged, boosted my morale, and had respect. Sometimes, I'd ask for the support I needed, and usually I got it. When I didn't, often I'd pick up my journal. Writing in my journal became a welcome, though sometimes painful, activity. In my journal, I always had a friend. Writing gave me a way to get things off my chest and express my thoughts and feelings.

May 6

As I learn to relax, I feel freer to think. Success to me means gaining a clearer picture of who I am and finding work that fits. By becoming more clear about my self-image, I'll realize more of my talents and powers.

I have more learning to do. I need to better recognize, confront, and manage my feelings. I'm still feeling hurt, but less afraid. I'm getting ready to begin networking. It's time to take other risks; I'll talk with John about next steps.

Another insight I had was that I had a choice: I could either put a lot of time into worrying, or I could take action. Oh, I worried about my finances running short before I found a job, about what the neighbors thought when they saw me out in the yard at midday, and about being accepted in the job market at forty-seven years old. But I noticed as I focused more on the present and on taking action, I worried less. For example, I began going to the library for at least two hours every day. The routine itself felt productive and energizing. The librarian, Mrs. Lingren, became one of my best advocates. When I asked her to direct me to the career resources section, she must have surmised that I'd been laid off. After I showed up at ten o'clock for the third morning in a row, she began to treat me as a regular. Our town library had a special reference and resource career section featuring directories and self-help books.

Eric, my management consultant friend, called one night. "Hi, Matt," he said. "If you haven't already read it, I wanted to suggest reading *Do What You Love, The Money Will Follow* by Marsha Sinetar.* You could ask your librarian if they have it. It focuses on paying attention to our inner wisdom in selecting work that is most fulfilling."

"You hit my hot button, Eric! Thanks for calling."

The next day I mounted the library steps two at a time.

"Good morning, Mrs. Lingren," I said.

"You look bright this morning," Mrs. Lingren replied.

"Mrs. Lingren, are you familiar with the book *Do What You Love . . .*"

Before I could complete the title she finished with ". . . *The Money Will Follow.*"

"Yes," I exclaimed, "by Marsha Sinetar."

---

*Marsha Sinetar, *Do What You Love, The Money Will Follow: Discovering Your Right Livelihood* (New York: Dell, 1987).

"It's been popular. I'm sorry to say that our copy has been checked out, but I know the bookstore in town carries it."

"Thanks, I'll pick it up this afternoon."

Mrs. Lingren hesitated and then said, "The headline in this morning's paper was 'Pink Slips Are Flying; 30,000 Laid Off Regionally.'"

"Mrs. Lingren, if I focus on the evening news and newspaper announcements, I'll get depressed and more afraid like so many others. No way! Even if many organizations *are* laying off workers, my twenty-odd years of experience tell me that some are always hiring."

"Yes, Matt, but I've talked with several others who have been laid off." Mrs. Lingren looked concerned.

I touched her on the shoulder. "Some of us are going to get jobs," I told her. "I plan to be one of them."

May 8

Marsha Sinetar's book was an affirmation that I was on the right course. I am convinced that my positive attitude will be necessary to find a meaningful job in this charged and challenging marketplace. At work I was known as a person who could solve a multitude of problems and materialize goals. I used to notice that the people on my staff with positive attitudes were the most flexible and effective. I'm ready to roll up my sleeves!

Lynda and I had just sat down for our after-dinner tea when the phone rang. A friendly voice said, "I hope I'm not disturbing you. This is John. I'd like to postpone tomorrow's meeting until next Thursday, the sixteenth."

I paused for a moment, then said, "Mmm, I had a lot to talk over with you. I'm a little disappointed."

"Sorry. One of my corporate clients has had an emergency." He paused, then continued, "How are things?"

"In fact, pretty good. I'm going to a career seminar at the community college on Thursday night."

"Sounds good. You sound positive."

"Yes, I've decided to begin networking this week."

"You're taking more action. Call me if you want to talk over strategy. See you next week."

I was always an early morning riser. My new daily routine involved a 6:30 run of three to six miles, coffee with Lynda, journal writing after breakfast, and the library from ten until twelve. I'd have lunch, and usually read the newspaper and take a walk until 1:30. During the afternoon, I'd read, work in the yard, sometimes meet with former colleagues or with a friend like George. I tried to keep the afternoons more flexible. Sometimes there'd be errands to do, but often I needed the time to collect my thoughts.

During this transitional period, Lynda was terrific most of the time. She rarely gave me the song and dance "You're not working, so you can do more of the household chores." We continued to share the chores. If she had one hot button, it was our finances. It would usually get triggered by specific events. A weekly occurrence seemed to be grocery shopping; we'd never had to watch our pennies, and now we were. Also, especially right after my job loss, declining invitations to the theater or to a restaurant in town was embarrassing for Lynda and sometimes instigated an argument between us. We both understood that making these adjustments was essential, but accepting them emotionally took time.

In spite of concerns about our finances, she primarily viewed this period as I did: a time for my self-discovery and for finding meaningful work. Because of her own career experience, she knew it took stamina and commitment to discover a meaningful path, and she applauded my courage. Most importantly, Lynda had faith, and she worked to be patient during this time. She'd often look at me and say, "Even though we're unsure about the future, you can't force things. Matt, *we* can't force things. Step by step is the way to go."

Lynda saw that my spirit was coming back. Even though I was out of work, I was beginning to feel better. When Lynda talked, I would genuinely listen, even though I didn't always like what I heard. When friends offered advice and feedback, I was interested in learning. I was becoming a voracious reader and was finding books, magazine articles, and other materials that were helpful. Taking a daily run and working in the yard became time invested in myself. I was learning to let go of some of my tension, which allowed for more creativity.

Passages
Do's and Don'ts

DO . . .

- Focus. Learn to be in the moment.
- Read self-help and inspirational books.
- Schedule library time.
- Continue writing in your journal.
- *Frequently* pause and evaluate what you've learned and your progress.

DON'T . . .

- Think that *you* have all the answers.
- Get discouraged as you sort out priorities.

May 9

I am struck by Margaret Fuller, the nineteenth-century literary critic: "For the sake of getting a living [we] forget to live." I certainly did. I can now see the extent of my unhappiness. I was working for an organization that really didn't believe in its people. I started to forget some of my own beliefs: that people can learn and improve, that people are trustworthy, that a company can be profitable and respect the lives of its employees. I will find an organization in which the leadership believes in its people. I want to become part of a team that promotes individual values as well as organizational health and productivity.

During this time, I constantly assessed my values. When I was a manager, I would frequently ask job candidates, "What do you value?" Now I asked the same of myself. Since I can remember, I've believed in treating others the way I like to be treated. I've valued follow-through and commitment. I've wanted to have fun at work; somehow this goal slipped away. Money was important, but it was not my master. Fundamentally, I valued having challenging work that I believed in and an environment that supported productivity and learning. I had seen myself in overlapping roles of leader, manager, and doer.

Now I wanted genuine support from an organization and a CEO who shared my values.

6

Flip-Flop

Opportunities and challenges

The career seminar was just four miles from my house. I left in plenty of time to arrive at 6:45 P.M. On the way I realized that I had not been so overwhelmed lately. In fact, I was doing pretty well at prioritizing and taking things step by step. There had been an engineering manager at Technology, Inc., who used to say, "I learned over the years to make chapter decisions." When we'd first worked together, he had created confusion by making everything a priority. Later, he said, "I learned to make one decision at a time and walk step by step . . . that way I'll trip a lot less."

I noticed the crowd was "dressed for success"—business suits and corporate elegance. I fit in well enough with my navy sport coat and slacks. There were many others scanning the room of about three hundred participants, looking for familiar faces and sizing up the competition. It seemed that this professional crowd had gotten the message "Act upbeat."

Promptly at seven the speaker walked onto the stage. She smiled at the size of the crowd. "Welcome," she said. "We are here for business." She asked, "How many of you have lost your jobs for one reason or another?" The majority raised their hands. "The message is clear: you are not alone." She continued. "As we begin a new decade, we can look back to see that an imaginary curtain was lowered, closing out the expansion and the growth of the eighties. When it was raised again, the stage was set for the current extremely competitive job market, which is now influenced by mergers, downsizing, a global arena, and an unpredictable economy. As companies restructure for survival and recalibrate for growth, one typical result is layoffs. Obviously, thousands of upper-level jobs have been eliminated, including those of manager, director, and vice president. And many of those laid off aren't coming back, at least in the foreseeable future. These positions comprise the career ladder many of you have known— the ladder most of you have climbed." There was complete silence, and many heads were nodding. She had everyone's attention.

"Layoffs and the looming atmosphere of dismissal in much of corporate America have left many of you feeling shocked, angry, trapped, lost, and betrayed," she continued. "Others of you have been relieved, sensing at some point you would have made a change anyway. Dismissal was the push some of you needed to get on with making that change sooner." Boy, was she talking my language! "Whether you're feeling shocked or relieved, the dominant theme in all of your lives is change."

She paused. "My name is Julia. Last year I was laid off from a bank where I was the manager of training and development. My primary focus was on individual career development and succession planning. Prior to this job I was a director of career planning with the state. After I was laid off, I went through a process of soul searching, clarifying my objective, learning to be flexible, and exploring different paths. My primary objectives were to do work I believed in and to have more control of my time. I wanted to be my own boss, so I became a career consultant and trainer. I went through much of what many of you are experiencing now. I can feel your concerns. I'm here to help you reconcile your past and move on to your futures." Julia looked about. "Does anyone have a question?"

A man stood up and, speaking for the crowd, asked, "Obviously many of us have been laid off. The media are constantly announcing that sales are sluggish, employment is shrinking, and people are cautious and depressed. How are we going to get jobs given the current state of affairs?"

"Yes, generally there is a slowdown," Julia responded. She

looked directly at the man, then scanned the room. She continued, "When compared with the past decade, the pace of progress has certainly changed. Change is the problem. It is also part of the solution. If you, as job seekers, are willing to change some of your conventional ways of thinking and learn difficult skills, you can win in the current challenging times."

Now, it seemed, she was talking specifically to me. "If you can identify and research individual and organizational problems, lead with a positive attitude, learn by treating every experience and every person as a teacher, improve on new behaviors, and remain flexible by trying different paths, then every one of you can win—even in this marketplace. All these success components and the current marketplace conditions point to leaving behind the career ladder strategy."

I thought about John's explanation of the career lattice approach. Julia was talking about the same concept.

Someone in the audience interjected, "What do you mean?"

"In the eighties many of us latched onto corporate career ladders. Like home run hitters, we leapt forward—up the ladder. Ten or fifteen years ago, how many of you began as indiviudal contributors, then advanced over this time to manager, director, vice president, or even president?"

Most hands were raised.

"Do you get my point? The direction was up, and the path was narrow. Corporate structures have shifted. It is no longer profitable or competitive to provide the same opportunities, especially at your levels. A career ladder suggests that there are only two ways to go: up or down. Up usually meant success, and down was the direction none of us wanted to go."

Julia paused as she turned to her blank flip pad. She wrote:

Self-management

"Self-management," she said. "Allow me to explain. This marketplace is calling for job seekers and career changers to manage their own careers. We cannot expect that any organization is going to guide us toward our next job or provide the all-too-familiar ten- or twenty-year security blanket. Many organizations are struggling to redirect and manage themselves. They are looking for people who have taken control of their own lives. Bottom line, they are asking, 'Can you boost our productivity and make us more competitive?' The same is the case if you choose to start a business. Customers will only buy if you are benefiting them. Self-management involves taking full responsibility for clarifying and prioritizing your skills and values and thoroughly researching the needs of organizations or the type of business that interests you."

A man spoke up, "How would you do this? In particular, I'm interested in working with a larger organization."

"One way, I believe, is to become a base hitter, not a home run slugger. Now, assuming that you know your next career objective, let's say you've targeted a particular company, one in which you'd like to interview." She began to write on the flip pad as she spoke. "Getting on base 1 involves in-depth company research; progressing to base 2 involves tailoring a marketing letter matching your experience, skills, and abilities with their needs; advancing to base 3 involves calling to follow up with the person to whom you addressed your marketing letter; and landing on base 4 — home plate — means securing a first interview. Here ends the first inning. In the second inning, the interviewing cycle, getting on base 1 represents a successful first interview, progressing to base 2 means a successful second interview, and so forth. Landing at home plate would be a successful final interview. You're still in the game. Next is the third inning — salary negotiations. Is this making sense to you?" On her flip pad, Julia had written:

Base hits!

Inning 1: Getting a first interview

1. Do in-depth company research
2. Tailor a marketing letter
3. Follow up calls
4. Decide on a time and place for a first interview

The same man questioned, "But why not go for the home run?"
"Do you mean, just call for an interview?"

"Yes. I've done that before."

"Today's market is extremely demanding, competitive. Look around you. Everyone here is looking for work and is talented in his or her own right! There are fewer obvious jobs. Organizations scrutinize more than ever. They must justify why their positions are open and closely examine each individual who becomes a candidate. Putting it simply, to become a candidate tomorrow, you've got to be prepared today. The best way I know to enhance the probability of your success is to take each inning step by step, or base by base."

A woman from the front row requested, "Can you give us an example of someone from a corporation who lost her job and then decided to start her own business? How would the self-management principles you mentioned apply in this situation?"

"I'm glad you asked that. Many examples come to mind. One woman I know climbed the rungs of the publishing business over the past sixteen years. She began as a sales representative, progressed to marketing manager, changed companies and shifted to editor, then became a senior editor. She was promoted again to the position of executive editor, and then vice president. Then, as she put it, 'I was ejected.' Her immediate response was to network through associates and colleagues for another senior editor position. Guess what? To put it mildly, the job market and economy had flip-flopped since her last job search. Staying on the same rung proved futile and moving up meant colliding with hundreds of competitors.

"Instead, she stepped back and took a look at her values, primary skills, what she *really* wanted and researched how the publishing business had changed. Her analysis revealed other ways of fulfilling her goal, including remaining in the publishing business and publishing materials that added value to people's lives. In short, she climbed off the familiar ladder and adopted a framework I discussed earlier called self-management."

Again, I thought, John would have called this framework a career lattice.

"Exploring a variety of new paths based on her values, skills, life needs, and marketplace changes, not on title, led her to open her own press, one dedicated to serving organizations and individuals conducting global trade. A global trade press — how timely.

I'd recently heard she had published a handbook on how to do business with Russia.

"In a nutshell," Julia summarized, "Whether you're looking to join a company or become self-employed, you've got to convince employers and customers that you can solve a problem for them. You've got to become part of the solution. In the fury of organizational restructuring, many of the rungs—positions—have become worn, broken, or obsolete. The woman publisher chose to reexamine and manage her assets and respect the changes in the marketplace. Her press provides solutions—vital information and expert guidance—for managers facing new worldwide business opportunities and cross-cultural challenges."

Ladder thinking, when the organization identifies the rung we should be on and pulls us up, is no longer to the point, I thought. As John would say, "A ladder no longer, but a lattice that works." Julia has just told us that it is each individual's responsibility to manage his or her mobility. It's like riding waves. The big surf of the eighties is down, and now we're out on our boards on smaller waves. I was pleased with my analogy.

We took a ten-minute break. I just stood up and stretched. We were scheduled to run until ten o'clock that evening.

After the break, Julia walked confidently to center stage and announced, "Let's get to work." The lights were dimmed, leaving a spotlight on her. Using a florescent red marker, she drew a huge hand on her newsprint flip pad. "We've all been dealt a special hand of talents and skills," she said, "every one of us. No one got a full deck, so don't worry about the rest of the fifty-two! It's important that you identify you own winning hand, then act using those talents and skills that most interest you. Talents are your special abilities or strengths; they are natural and inherited, like the color of your hair or eyes. We all know people, including ourselves, who are natural athletes but who cannot carry a tune, or people who write naturally but would fall short as a computer programmer. Skills, on the other hand, are things we learn to do in order to live our lives and perform our jobs. For example, you can become skilled at typing, building houses, appraising property, or cooking. Having personally been through the transition that every one of you is going through, I believe this

BIG waves—growth sectors—
are receding

SMALLER waves—and pinpoint
niches—are developing

is a time for self-renewal. One way to renew yourselves and find meaningful work is to discover your natural talents and to clar-ify the skills you want to use in your next job." She labeled each finger with one of her own talents and skills, which were public speaking, analyzing, creating ideas, influencing, and pioneering.

"Now, I'd like every one of you to do the same. First, trace one of your hands on the blank paper in your folders. Next, label each finger—and your thumb—with your talents and skills. Re-lax for a moment and write what comes to mind. Then on the worksheet in your packet titled 'Summary of Top Talents and Skills,' prioritize your talents and skills from most to least im-portant. Please remember, this is a learning and discovery process. As you learn about yourselves during this transition, some of you

---

Prioritizing Top Talents and Skills

Instructions: On a separate piece of paper, brainstorm—list as many of your talents and skills as possible. On this page, drawing from the list you've made, write down your five top talents and skills. Then, rank order your three top ones.

Note: This exercise will be helpful later on in developing your resumé, expressing your capabilities and accomplishments, and interviewing. You may decide that you have three top talents *and* three top skills (possibly more) that you want to bring to your next job. In this case, prioritize each.

Five Top Talents and Skills

1. _____
2. _____
3. _____
4. _____
5. _____

Three Top Talents and Skills

1. _____
2. _____
3. _____

---

will confirm what you've written, and others will reassess their talents and skills." The lights brightened.

After twenty minutes, Julia asked how many had labeled three or four fingers. Most hands were raised. "The point is that you all have talents and skills," she said. "Look around you! I encourage all of you to use what comes *naturally* and to bring the skills that you *want* to use into this huge job marketplace. By the way, how many of you thought this exercise was difficult? Mmm, I agree. I found naming my talents and skills a challenge—and it's an on-going one. Deciding which talents and skills I wanted to really bring to the marketplace was the toughest part. By persevering in analyzing my past experiences—the skills and talent they involved and how I felt about them—networking, and gathering marketplace information, I finally put it together."

A young man spoke up, "Why prioritize our talents and skills?"

"Prioritizing helps us to focus. Rarely are all of our values, interests, or talents and skills of equal importance. You may want to reserve the use of some of your talents and skills for activities outside of work. Why manage more than you have to? Manage what is most important to you—those talents and skills you want to bring to your work."

Next, Julia encouraged us to write down situations in which we had applied our talents and skills. For example, after recounting some of my past work activities, I labeled one of my fingers "planning," since I seemed to have a natural ability to make arrangements for distant goals and to follow through. As an example of my ability to plan, I wrote:

> Planned and organized four divisional steering committee meetings resulting in the redevelopment of our operating principles.

I realized this was a way for all of us to reclaim our abilities. I could see how I might use much of this workshop to rewrite a stronger, results-oriented resumé.

The first hour of the workshop was spent talking about self-management in a changed economy. During the second hour, we did exercises related to talents and skills. In the final hour, Julia focused on goal setting, planning, and other job-search strategies. Throughout she emphasized creating short-term results, "base hits," which would eventually define and add up to our future goals. For instance, these base hits might be making five network calls every day, or sending a tailored marketing letter to a vice president, or scheduling a meeting with a contact who would be able to give information on what it's like to work for a smaller business, or hand writing a thank-you note.

Julia ended the workshop by saying, "You all have qualities of distinction; self-management begins with clarifying these qualities. You've got to know what you have to manage. Good luck."

As the crowd filed out of the auditorium, people looked loaded down with information, as if they were digesting a big meal. It was time to go home, get a good night's rest, then sort things out in the morning.

The dirt path that went through the woods behind our house was my favorite place to run. I was out on the trail early the next morning, feeling motivated. My feet were cushioned by the packed trail, and I imagined I was a pioneer scout moving swifty and silently through the woods. I remembered Julia's words: "Focus on today, make a weekly plan, and you'll achieve your goals." Another one of the worksheets that she gave us was a "Weekly Planner." The morning sun flickered through the spruces and pines, every so often its rays catching my face. The smell of spring and the chirping birds were a gift. I thought, This outdoor environment suits me. I'll just *know* when a work culture fits. Julia was right. Everyone's winning edge is knowing his or her own truth. My journey is to rediscover my natural talents and find an environment that's a comfortable match. I want to express myself, not just play to an audience.

Next week I would begin networking. I needed first-hand information about the current marketplace. I planned to begin calling people from my past and then make new contacts.

We went to the fine arts museum that weekend, a welcome treat. Lynda and I enjoy Impressionist painting. As we strolled, Lynda remarked, "Taking a rest from your job search is important."

"Funny," I said, "the presenter at the career seminar said the same thing. She called it gaining perspective."

Lynda added, "For example, at the collaborative when trying to solve a design problem, I might hit a snag. Often, by simply taking a walk, the solution appears."

"You know, Lynda, I really understand what you mean. When I got close to that Renoir, things became a blur. I needed to step back to see the full picture."

May 13

I need to pace myself—I'm running a marathon, not a quarter-mile race. Spending time with Lynda and visiting Chris are a source of sustenance. They have supported me through some testing times. I can still establish a rigorous job-search campaign and also make time for myself and my family. Balance essentially involves management. I'm going to manage my days, weeks, and probably months so I can derive optimal benefit for my efforts.

Weekly Planner

Week from _____ to _____

Priority Calls	Networking Calls	To Do

Priority Calls

1. _____

Note: _____

2. _____

Note: _____

3. _____

Note: _____

4. _____

Note: _____

_____

Networking Calls

1. _____

Note: _____

2. _____

Note: _____

3. _____

Note: _____

4. _____

Note: _____

_____

To Do

1. _____

2. _____

3. _____

4. _____

5. _____

6. _____

7. _____

8. _____

9. _____

Appointments

1. _____

Note: _____

2. _____

Note: _____

3. _____

Note: _____

4. _____

Note: _____

_____

Marketing Calls

1. _____

Note: _____

2. _____

Note: _____

3. _____

Note: _____

4. _____

Note: _____

_____

Notes

_____

_____

_____

_____

Personal To Do

_____

_____

Planning notes for the future: _____

_____

_____

Flip-Flop
Do's and Don'ts

DO . . .

- Attend workshops and career seminars.
- Project a professional self-image.
- Accept responsibility for your transition.
- Understand the changes in the job market.
- Go for base hits.
- Acknowledge your special talents.
- Prioritize your skills and write down examples of them.
- Keep some balance in your life—spend time with your friends and family; have fun on the weekends.
- Pace yourself; you're running a marathon.

DON'T . . .

- Close your mind to new ideas.
- Take responsibility for what you're not in control of—such as, the economy or other people.
- Sit passively in workshops; do the exercises with gusto!
- Try to make sense of all your new lessons at once.

May 14

Lynda has thoughtfully copied on the phone message pad a line from Robert Fulghum's book, "Live a balanced life. Learn some and think some and draw and paint and sing and dance and play and work every day some."* Thank you Robert Fulghum and Lynda.

*Robert Fulghum, All I Really Need to Know I Learned in Kindergarten (New York: Villard Books, 1988).

Ways to Stay Balanced

- Step back when stuck on a problem.

- After making several networking calls, be patient when waiting for return calls.

- Take a deep breath between phone calls.

- Get an answering machine to screen calls, so as to stay focused when reading or writing.

- Give a helping hand to a colleague who is job searching.

7

Gateways

Open sez me!

Monday, after my second cup of coffee, I looked over my notes on Julia's class. She had talked about networking and how to do it right. I knew this was the next step for me.

Many of my colleagues seemed pessimistic about networking, but Maria, my human resource manager friend, once said, "Networking became my professional lifeline when I was out of work." I reviewed the basic and helpful principles for networking Julia had given us and wrote these down as networking guidelines.

Back at Technology, Inc., I recalled, we had hired Qualtec, a total quality management (TQM) consultancy, to train us in facilitating effective work teams. The system they trained us on was called PAL, which stood for purpose, agenda, and limit. The system gave each work team structure and promoted independence and productivity.

A light went on! Since I wanted to create some structure and be productive, why not use PAL for my own networking? I grabbed a pad and sketched out how I might do it.

P   Purpose: The aim of my call or meeting.

A   Agenda: A list of topics to be discussed. I could have one or two topics in mind.

L   Limit: The amount of time I'd spend talking and/or meet-
                 ing with someone. Also, if it's a meeting, the place.

During the next three days, I set a goal that I would call twenty contacts and would set up meetings with at least seven. PAL helped me maximize my probability for success by keeping me focused and organized. It allowed me to let the contact know that I wouldn't waste his or her time or confuse the information gathering by asking for a job. It also functioned as an inanimate support on my Life, Inc., board.

I designed a PAL contact form: an 8½ × 11 sheet of copy paper that could be duplicated and used as a worksheet and record. As I networked, I clipped this contact form into a three-ring binder. I arranged the contact forms according to discipline—bio-tech, health care, software—and alphabetically by last name.

I also created a "PAL card," writing a summary of the PAL

Networking Guidelines

1. Set goals and schedule networking time.

2. Begin every day by calling someone you've talked with in the past.

3. Start by talking with people you know.

4. Distinguish between information networking and job interview networking. Let your contact know up front which of these you seek.

5. Ask each contact for one or two more names.

6. Join a support group for the purpose of reporting the results of your efforts, gathering additional information, and helping others.

7. Stay open to surprises.

8. Reward yourself for your learning and successes.

The PAL System for Networking

Name: _____   Date: _____

Profession: _____   Telephone: _____

Company: _____   Referred by: _____

Address: _____

_____

PAL

Purpose:
My aim in calling you is _____

_____

_____

Agenda:
Specifically, I'd like to
know or discuss _____

_____

_____

Limit:
I'm asking for _____
minutes of your time _____

Results

Meeting (date/time/place): _____

Telephone call (date/time/number): _____

Follow-up (when): _____

Notes and ideas: _____

_____

_____

Closure: _____

program on the back of one of my Technology, Inc., business cards. I carried this card in my wallet and used it as a quick reference when making calls when I wasn't in my office at home, for example in between interviews or when I was at the library and needed to make a call.

When I made a call, I'd state my purpose, for example: "My aim in calling you is to talk to a successful person who has moved from management into TQM consulting." Then I'd indicate my agenda, for instance: "Specifically, I'd like to discuss the skills you currently use and what your personal rewards are." Finally, I'd tell my contact the time limit: "I'm asking for thirty minutes of your time, on a date and at a place convenient to you."

PAL Card

PAL

Purpose: My aim in calling you is . . .

Agenda: Specifically, I'd like to know or discuss . . .

Limit: I'm asking for _____ minutes of your time.

Thank You

On my contact form I'd also log the results of my conversation, including the meeting time and place, follow-up information, and any notes and ideas. Sometimes I wasn't able to arrange a face-to-face meeting. Then I'd try to schedule a telephone conversation on a date and at a time convenient to the contact.

A gracious thank you was the way I closed every PAL conversation and meeting. After a telephone conversation, saying thank you was usually enough. If the person was exceptionally helpful, I'd ask for their address and send a friendly note. After a meeting, I'd send a handwritten note or a typed letter, depending on the tenor of our meeting.

One of my first network calls was to Jerry Brine, a colleague and vice president of operations who had been caught in a company layoff.

The receptionist answered, saying, "Mr. Brine's office. May I help you?"

I said, "Yes, this is Matt Townden. May I talk with Jerry?"

The receptionist asked, "Is Mr. Brine expecting your call?"

I thought for a second and replied, "No, but I know Jerry well. We worked together in the past."

"Just one moment, I have another call coming in."

She was back in a minute and said, "Please give me your name again. Thank you. I'm going to place you on hold."

After a bit, Jerry picked up. "Matt! Hello, stranger."

"Good to hear your voice, Jerry. You know, I've been busy." I paused for a moment and said, "I don't want to take your time now, Jerry, but I've been laid off."

Jerry immediately sympathized, "Sorry to hear that. I know that one."

"Jerry," I said, "my purpose in calling you is to talk with someone I respect who landed another job in this tough market. I'm really interested in learning about networking from you."

"Matt, I'm flattered you asked. I've found a company that's a good fit, and I'd be happy to tell you how I did it. How about lunch next week? My secretary can set it up."

"Great. See you next week. Oh, by the way, what's your secretary's name?"

"Lisa. See you next week."

The week was flying by. I had changed my daily routine to accommodate my networking efforts. Now, I was going to the library three times a week. Reaching people between eight and nine, twelve and one, and four and six seemed to work best. These are the hours when secretaries aren't there, meetings don't occur, and busy people answer their own phones. I still ran in the morning, usually ate lunch after I made my noontime calls, and was typically on the phone when Lynda arrived home from work. Lynda knew my schedule, and if she needed to, she could usually reach me during the day.

On Thursday, I met with John as usual. As I walked into the office he said, "Let's exchange chairs. If you'd like, sit over here." As I sat, facing the opposite way, above John's head I could see on the wall a quote by Mozart that I hadn't noticed before.

I cannot write poetically, for I am no poet. I cannot artfully arrange my phrases so as to give light and shade. Neither am I a painter; nor can I even express my thoughts by gesture and pantomime, for I am no dancer. But I can do so in sounds. I am a musician.

"John," I commented, "that quote is about self-expression."
"Yes, it is."
"Sitting in this chair has given me another perspective. I'll remember this as a metaphor for looking at things from different angles."
"That's what the lattice approach is about." John paused.
"Mmm."
"The lattice approach is about taking responsibility, about discovering and managing your own path, not the path an organization or another individual chooses for you."
"Ah, I get it. Like the ivy; it chooses its own path and finds its way."
John smiled and said, "That makes for a healthy plant."
I smiled back and commented, "And a happy one, too."
We talked about my networking efforts using PAL and how my primary focus at this point was information. John agreed. I told him about my first network call, to a colleague who had been

determined to find a leadership position as senior vice president of operations and had done so. During the call, my colleague had mentioned that he had found a "natural fit." "Tell me," said John, "What would be a natural fit for you?" I looked up, visualizing my "special hand of talents." Then I said, "I want to help people and an organization grow and be productive. My natural talents include leadership, presenting ideas, planning, consulting, and managing. For the past several years I've missed working in an environment where people are trusted and the culture is open to learning. I need diversity in my work, and I believe others do as well."

John looked pleased and said, "Matt, I think you're turning the corner. You can continue to deal with your feelings and handle your job search as well. You're ready to gather marketplace information and find your spot."

"Yes, to express myself and choose my own path."

I paused for a moment, reflecting on my first session with John and those first several weeks of being laid off, then continued. "I remember when we first met, I had tears in my eyes and a feeling like lead in my stomach. What a contrast between the way I felt then and the way I feel now."

"As we said in our first session, things change. You have changed and will continue to do so."

"I'm beginning to see that. It's not easy to change. I still feel those tears and sometimes the lead."

"Often, you'll still have those feelings. You've gone through a traumatic period. You're in transition, and you're still facing many unknowns."

I murmured my agreement.

"Remember, Matt, just because you're making progress doesn't mean you're devoid of feelings."

"Well, that's right."

"You're still working through your hurt."

"I guess I'll continue to do so for a while."

"On another note, I want to encourage you to continue to define your talents and to document your observations about organizations you visit. Clarity is a powerful tool.

"Have you thought about people you admire?" John went on.

I mentioned that I had written about Mother Teresa and Winston Churchill because they had the vision and the conviction to stick with what they believed.

"Is there anyone in industry who has the kind of conviction you admire?"

"Yes, there is. Ken Olson, founder and former CEO of Digital Equipment Corporation. He had the faith and courage to grow a world-renowned computer company and treat his employees well, even during downsizing."

John reached over and pulled a book off the shelf. John said, "This is *The Age of Unreason* by Charles Handy, one of my favorite books.* Warren Bennis wrote the foreword, in which he says 'Charles Handy's book is about the story of our time: change.' It is not only important to clarify your values but to define the characteristics of a job that would foster your success. Mr. Handy addresses this issue by talking about the 'inverted doughnut.'"

"Sounds like something good to eat!"

"It could be! Basically, the point of his analogy is that the core of the doughnut represents the job description, the part of a job that is clearly defined."

"You mean the have-to-do's?"

"Yes."

"The rest of the inverted doughnut, in this case the space, consists of the tasks and responsibilities that are not clearly defined, that go beyond the job description. For some people, like a typist or toll taker, the doughnut is mostly all core or job description with very little space for initiative. Do you know what I'm driving at?"

"I think so. In my case too much core would drive me crazy. I like looking for opportunities and using my creativity."

"Yes, Matt, I think you've got it. Here's a handout called 'The Inverted Doughnut.' It further describes this principle. Please look it over and use this worksheet to draw your own inverted doughnut. Label the characteristics that make up your core and your space."

"Sounds interesting."

---

*Charles E. Handy, *The Age of Unreason* (Boston: Harvard Business School Press, 1990).

The Inverted Doughnut

Core: Job description
Space: Tasks and responsibilities that
go beyond the job description

Core: Little definition;
always more that could
be done.
Space: Huge amount of
opportunity for initiative.

Position: Caring
professional,
marketing and
sales representative,
entrepreneur

Core: Larger, more
defined job description.
Space: Balance between
job requirements and
undefined opportunity.

Position: Manager,
CEO, president,
individual contributor
(many of these
positions exist in
most organizations)

Core: Mostly all core;
tight job description.
Space: Very little initiative
and creativity needed.

Position: Typist, word
processor, toll taker,
bank teller

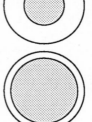

Instructions: First, draw the "doughnut" that best represents you
in your last job. How much core (job definition) did you have? How
much space (room for opportunity) did you have? Next, draw the
"doughnut" that best represents what you want now. How much
core do you want? How much space do you want?

Note: Your doughnut can *change* at different times in your life.
Compare the past and present, and think about the differences
and similarities in your goals. You can also discuss your findings
at informational interviews, a great way to prepare for interviews!

Doughnut representing
last job:

Doughnut representing
what you want now:

SOURCE: The Inverted Doughnut; p. 129 from Charles E. Handy,
The Age of Unreason (Boston: Harvard Business School Press,
1990). Copyright © 1989 by Charles Handy. Foreword © 1990
by the President and Fellows of Harvard College. Used with
permission of the publishers.

At the end of our session I told John about my plans to diligently network and reassured him that I was continuing to write in my journal about what work would feel natural.

I had just got home and was standing at the front door, fishing for my house keys, when the phone started ringing. I turned the latch and heard the message machine recording. "Matt, how's it going?" Immediately I recognized my accountant's friendly voice.

I grabbed the receiver and said, "I'm fine, Russ. I was just walking in."

"How's the job search? Is the financial plan still working?" he asked.

"Lynda and I have been sticking to our budget. Sometimes it's not easy. We've gotten into a couple of spats over expenses, nothing major. When I get a job, I've told her we're going to pick a nice restaurant and celebrate."

"That's the spirit!"

"Russ, I've got a couple of network calls scheduled, so I need to go. But I greatly appreciate your concern."

"No problem."

I was just about to say good-bye when I thought of networking through Russ.

"Russ, just a second. I mentioned that I've been networking. If you can think of one of your company contacts I should be talking with, would you let me know?"

"Sure, any specific area you're interested in?"

"Glad you asked. My interest is in internal or external consultants in the total quality management area. Most of these folks would be working with progressive organizations."

"I understand. I recently read an article in *Fortune* about quality. All the companies from McDonald's to GM are pitching quality these days."

"You've got the picture. Thanks for watching."

After we hung up, I thought, Russ will call if he thinks of anyone. When I get the job I want, I'm going to ask Russ and his wife to join Lynda and me for a celebration dinner. We'll all enjoy that.

Mrs. Lingren would probably miss me at the library, but I had a networking interview set up for twelve with my colleague Jerry Brine, the vice president of operations at Capital, Inc. When I arrived in Jerry's office, he looked content. His office was on the twentieth floor and overlooked the gold statehouse dome. In the distance, the glistening river was dotted with white sails darting back and forth. What a view! We both faced the window, exchanging pleasantries, observing and commenting on the city and river view.

As we took the elevator to the company dining room, Jerry explained that the dining room, up until a year before, had been open only to senior managers and other "mucky mucks." "Opening the thirtieth floor to all employees," Jerry continued, "was part of our total quality leadership commitment." More like an equality commitment, I thought. "Sounds like progress," I said. I stuck with my agenda and asked Jerry, "What made you a successful networker?"

"Let me see. First, I had a very clear, strong vision to become a leader in another corporation. I wanted to be able to influence the direction of the next company I joined. I've talked to other successful networkers who have not been as clear about their career goal, but they were clear that they were meeting to gather information."

"Mmmm. You mean they weren't meeting to ask for or interview for a job?"

"Right." Jerry continued, "One of my strategies was to talk with as many senior-level executives in organizations, both medium and large, as I could find. Often, after I'd read about executives in magazines like *Inc., Fortune, Newsweek,* and the *Wall Street Journal,* I'd give them a call. On occasion, one of the articles had been written by one of these execs."

"Sounds like a great idea."

"I met with seven or eight executives using this method, including two presidents. I wasn't always clear about what the outcome of our meetings would be, but meeting with them like this seemed to be okay. Talking about their concerns and accomplishments would inevitably heighten their interest in helping me."

Jerry paused for a moment, took a bite out of his sandwich, and asked, "How's the fish?"

"It's good. I've been listening to you, so I hardly noticed."

"The food is okay here. The best part is the view!"

"The view is special."

"Matt, when networking with those executives, one thing I learned was to become open to surprises."

"What do you mean?"

"Frequently, as we conversed, either they or I would come up with suggestions and ideas I hadn't anticipated. For instance, one exec suggested that I write a letter to one of his board members expressing my interests. At another meeting, I noticed hanging on the wall an article 'Timely Approaches to the Global Market- place' the exec had written that had been published by one of the national business magazines. He had said he had written it as a means of gaining recognition in his organization, hoping it would aid in his advancement to senior vice president. From this I got the idea of writing an article to gain recognition in the marketplace for job-hunting purposes. Readers of my article might call me for more information, which would expand my network and possibly lead to job interviews. I complimented the execu- tive on his accomplishment, and told him my idea, and asked that he introduce me to the magazine's editors. He agreed, thinking that this would help me get my name out there."

I responded, "So you can't really predict outcomes."

"No, not at all. Meet people, get into conversations . . . stay open to surprises!

"Matt!" Jerry exclaimed, "let me tell you something." I leaned forward. "Networking led me to meet 150 people face to face in five months. I also wrote 500 letters inquiring about jobs, describing my background, and saying thank you. Organization was imperative; I kept precise records of all contacts and meet- ings. All of this effort finally, within five months, led me to the job I wanted. One networking success led to another, even though the process did get tiring at times." Jerry smiled, then said, "For inspiration, I put a sign on my home office wall and one on my car's sun visor that read 'I will get a *leadership* position in a cor- poration.'" Jerry was filled with pride and energy as he told his story. He went on, "Now that I have a job, I still continue to network. I stay connected to people, informed of changes, and aware of shifts in my profession."

"That's a great story."

"Thanks, Matt. I wanted to emphasize the importance of gathering current information regarding your profession and what companies are looking for when they hire. Both you and I have discovered that things never stay the same."

"Yeah, we found that out the hard way!"

"Here are a couple of questions I learned to ask, especially of networking contacts I considered colleagues."

"Why colleagues?"

"Because they usually worked in the positions and companies in which I had interest. I'll tell you the questions, then explain further. First, I'd ask, 'What are some of the things that you *do* that make you successful in your job? Could you give me some specific examples?' Second, I'd ask, 'What are some of the skills and personality qualities that make you successful in your job?' Depending on the person, if this question seemed too personal, I'd ask, 'If you were to hire someone today, for a similar position to yours, what are some of the skills and personality qualities you'd look for?'"

I wrote these questions down as Jerry talked.

"Those sound like terrific questions. Why exactly would you ask them of colleagues?"

"Remember, I said my interest was to land a leadership position?"

Networking Questions

1. What are some of the things that you do that make you successful in your job? Could you give me some specific examples?

2. What are some of your skills and personality qualities that make you successful?

   An alternative to number 2:

3. If you were to hire someone for a position similar to yours, what are some of the skills and personality qualities you'd look for?

"I do."

"Well, I'd ask these questions specifically to colleagues who were in leadership positions because I wanted to get the most current information concerning what they *did* and the *qualities* they possessed that made them successful. After asking these questions of several colleagues, I began to see a pattern of how and why successful people in my profession achieved results. They were successful because of particular things they *did* and *qualities* they had. Regarding your professional goals, I'm sure you're already aware of some of these things, but you'll become more aware and up-to-date."

"How would you apply this information to job interviewing?"

"Good question. I'd list and then compare the skills and qualities I had with those similar to the ones of successful people in my profession. Next, I'd write down examples, things I had done, that were illustrative of these skills and qualities. This was all in preparation for interviewing. When that time came, I felt more confident and prepared to share information based on my current marketplace research."

"I see. You know, this is just a thought, but I can also see that by asking these questions, you could also identify skills you may have needed to improve in order to achieve your goal. For example, in my case, say my goal is external consulting, and after questioning colleagues, I discovered a desirable skill was selling, I'd probably need to take a course in this area."

"Good point, that's another application, one I overlooked."

"Jerry, your ideas are great. Better yet, you've tested them." I took a sip of coffee, then asked, "Before we end, are there any last suggestions you could give me?"

"Mmmm . . . If you'll bear with me, I'll continue to use myself as an example. Even though I was focused, I saw networking as a process. When I'd meet someone, I'd say to myself, 'This person, somehow, is a link toward my goal,' not this person *has* to have the answer or they *must* have a job for me. This meant it was mostly up to me to figure out what there was to learn from each meeting. From there, I would evaluate how this learning might add value to my search. If I'd used the other tack, trying to force answers and results, I'd have felt defeated in no time."

Jerry was providing me with a terrific example of perseverance and focus and also of balance. He was basically saying that net-working was a process of continually meeting people for the pur-poses of clarifying what you wanted and for figuring out what they — customers and companies — wanted. Part of my challenge was staying on the path. If I did, eventually I'd make a match.

One of our differences was that I would have considered part-time work as a stepping-stone to a full-time position, and Jerry would not have. Before I left, we stopped back at his office. Jerry pulled a worksheet, "Networking: The Active Use of Contacts," from his files and handed it to me. As I drove home, I kept think-ing, Jerry seems happy. His office has a great view!

During the week I exceeded my goal, arranging eight network meetings after making twenty calls. The PAL approach gave structure to the process. In every phone conversation, I'd think about getting a base hit! I learned to put more energy into listening and asking questions instead of thinking how to manipulate the person into spending some time with me. What to say next would emerge from my questions and their answers. I had less time for running, but I learned to take a quick break by looking out the window in our office that faced the woods and then imagining myself running along the path. By Tuesday, May 21, I had met with three network contacts in addition to Jerry, one from a con-sulting firm and the other two from banking and high tech. "The marketplace," Julia had said, "is solution based and results ori-ented." This was being confirmed by my contacts. Clearly, my approach of listening, asking questions if I didn't understand, and basically sticking to my agenda was netting results. Always, I'd graciously ask for other contacts, and sometimes these were forth-coming.

But there were often moments I felt discouraged. My journal writing helped me tell that side of the story.

May 20

I'm forty-seven years old. I've got great ideas, but who's going to hire me? They want younger people, just like the company that laid me off. Now, I'm generalizing because I'm feeling down. I guess I'm entitled to the down times as well.

Mrs. Lingren is very supportive. The other day she said, "Persevere. Find the right company and you'll soar. You'll be <u>good</u> for each other."

Networking: The Active Use of Contacts

Instructions: List all the people you know in each category. Then call or write them for information.

Business executives/owners	Past business associates	Clergy	Politicians, civic and community leaders
College professors, deans, presidents	College alumni, fraternity/sorority members	Salespeople	Doctors, therapists
Consultants	Insurance/stock market representatives	Friends	Others

I want to focus more on all the positive feedback I've been getting—not my fear. Lynda had a good suggestion. I'll call George to ask him about referring me to a job-search support group.

Typically, for me, in the morning, things looked more clear. I had more perspective, like stepping back from an Impressionist painting, as I'd learned the other day. Curiosity led me to investigate the lives of people who were leaders, developers, and lifelong learners. Reading stories about and biographies on people like Buckminster Fuller, an inventor, educator, and architect; Armand Hammer, the vital millionaire industrialist; and Norman Vincent Peale, the best-selling author of *The Power of Positive Thinking*, inspired me to persevere.*

George called me late Tuesday afternoon, just as I was picking up the phone to call back a network contact. He's such a great friend. He listens, he's rarely judgmental, and he genuinely wants to help. George asked, "Matt, what are you doing tonight?"

"I don't have plans."

"Well, I know of a leaderless support group that is meeting for the first time tonight. They're looking for a fourth member."

"This must be what is meant by serendipity."

The purpose of a leaderless support group is to help every member gain mastery identifying and accomplishing his or her goals. Our group was composed of four members, each in a different line of work. All the members heard about the group through networking.

I arrived at Frank's, the host for the evening, at 7:15. As I opened my car door, another car pulled into the drive. The driver, a young woman of about thirty, introduced herself as Betty and asked if I was there for the group. Frank met us at the door and greeted us with "Welcome." The fourth member was sitting on the living room sofa, petting a contented golden retriever. She introduced herself as Jackie. "I'm Matt," I replied. "It's nice to be here."

At the first meeting, we agreed to meet once a week, on Tues-

*Norman Vincent Peale, *The Power of Positive Thinking* (New York: Prentice-Hall, 1952).

day evenings promptly at 7:30. Another decision was to take turns offering our homes as meeting places and to serve soft drinks only — this was no party! We also established a procedure. For the first five minutes we would exchange pleasantries, then it would be time for business. All information shared by members would be held in confidence.

This is how our group worked. Within a five-minute time frame, Jackie, for example, would present her problem or challenge. Then, for fifteen minutes she would receive feedback and questions from others. Group members took turns keeping track of the time for one another.

Within the first twenty minutes, Jackie had presented her issues and gotten feedback. Frank volunteered to present next. Our procedure showed all of us that we could be concise and responsive and get things done. Time was precious. This was meant to be a supportive and productive meeting for all four members. We decided our future meetings would run from 7:30 to 9:00, although during our first meeting we had allowed extra time to get acquainted. We also decided that at the end of each meeting, we would spend five minutes to confirm the next meeting and say good-byes.

Between group meetings, members agreed we would call one another for support and meet to do research or any other activity that would help advance us toward our individual goals.

On the way home, I thought, Our group is small and quite diverse, but we are assembled for a common purpose — to support one another in finding work that we wanted in the shortest amount of time possible. Frank had been an architect; he was also a divorced father with two children. He literally had had to sell his home to make ends meet. Betty had been a C.P.A.; she was black and had moved to this area to take a job. Little did she know that six months later she'd be laid off. One of her biggest issues was being separated from her family. In her words, "I moved for the adventure, but I didn't know what price I'd have to pay. But I guess this is part of it, I'm going to stick it out. I've joined this group for support." The third member, Jackie, had been a department store manager at a high-priced retailer. To her disappointment, the clientele she had built was now responding to

---

Leaderless Group Guidelines

- Ideally, involve four to six members.

- Meet at one another's homes.

- Serve soft drinks only—this is not a party.

- Allow five minutes for each member to present her or his issue(s).

- Each member should get twenty minutes of feedback from the group.

- Begin on time, and end on time.

- Support one another between meetings.

- If members agree, the rules are made to be broken!

---

the sluggish economy—shopping "off-price." Living with her parents, her plans to move were cut short, due to a massive company layoff.

All members were in career transition and each seemed motivated and helpful. They were just the group I needed to help me check out my ideas and achieve my goals. The night was clear, the Big Dipper was sparkling, *and* I had the green light at the five-way intersection!

Friday morning I was off to the city again to meet with Margaret, a quality improvement manager responsible for customer service. I was especially interested in learning about her work advising managers and vice presidents on how to improve work methods and productivity. I could see myself in the same role in the future.

As I drove, I thought about what I liked about total quality management. TQM is an improvement process that allows companies to meet both their customer needs and the individual needs of their employees in a mutually beneficial way. This win/win process eventually leads to increased productivity and customer satisfaction. I think it was the chairman of IBM who said, "Satisfied customers are the only reason we are in business."

Margaret's office had another beautiful view overlooking the bay side of the city. Starting a meeting by looking out the windows had its advantages. We got acquainted as we appreciated the skyline. The office was spacious, with an informal seating area near the window and a desk and computer across from the seating area.

Margaret invited me to sit down and then began, "Fundamentally, our CEO's philosophy is to look continually at improving the way we do things. He trusts his employees will develop and improve on reliable methods to meet customers' needs."

"Oh, so improvement, continuous improvement, is a company value," I commented.

"Yes, individual and organizational learning can never stop." We went on, discussing together how this philosophy influenced sales, customer service, product development, and selection.

As Margaret talked, I felt both excited and relaxed. She was confirming for me that there were organizations that were concerned about learning as well as about being competitive in today's global market.

For a couple of moments, I thought, Things are going pretty well; maybe I'll ask Margaret if there's a job opening in TQM with her company. Quickly recalling the original intent of my networking call, I remembered we had agreed to meet for informational purposes *only*. I stuck with the agreement. It's so tempting, when you're aching for work, to cross that line—that fragile line. But break that line, and you may lose a valuable contact for yourself and others. Stick with your agenda. You can call at a later date to inquire about jobs.

Back on track, I thought about the networking questions Jerry Brine had introduced me to. Here was an opportunity, with a colleague, to better understand what a quality manager does and what qualities she had that contributed to her success.

"Margaret, you seem to enjoy what you do, and obviously you've been successful in a highly competitive industry and marketplace."

"Thank you. I like to think so."

"Do you mind if I ask you a question in regard to your success?"

"Um . . . sure."

I sat back and said, "This is the question. What are some of the things you *do* that make you successful in your job?"

"Hmmm. It isn't often that I get asked a question like that."

I nodded and said, "Could you give me some specific examples? I'm trying to learn what makes TQM professionals successful in today's marketplace."

"Well, I read constantly, if that's what you mean. Because I'm so busy, I usually read articles. I subscribe to the *Journal for Quality and Participation.* Also, I'm a member of ASQC."

"This is exactly what I mean. What is ASQC?"

"Oh, the American Society for Quality Control, a nonprofit organization. I look to them for information and tools. They have thousands of members and hundreds of corporations that belong."

"I'll bet they're also a good networking source."

"They are for me, especially for information! Regarding my specific job," she continued, "I make it a point to meet with the president at least twice a month. Also, I call him whenever I need to. His buy-in and our collaboration on processes and programs are essential to our successful TQM effort."

"That's been my experience; acceptance and participation from the top are essential."

"On a regular basis, I facilitate meetings with all division heads to discuss what is and is not working in our quality program. I use the word *facilitate* because I ask a lot of questions, as opposed to taking a know-it-all position."

"That's a good one to remember. You facilitate meetings by asking questions."

"Another thing, and this builds on the last point. I always respect who I'm working with. I ask before I judge. Part of my role is to demonstrate the behavior I expect of others. Change is rarely easy for anybody. I want to find out why someone acted the way they did. They usually have a good reason, and often I learn something."

"You stay open to learning."

"Yes, I listen to others. That brings me to the issues of trust and patience. I trust that if we confront, rather than run from, problems, we'll resolve them eventually. Often, part of the process involves conflict among divisions or specific team members. I encourage people to talk about their differences. I'm also patient.

If our goals are to increase customer service and gain competitive advantage, identifying nonvaluing practices and implementing better ones takes time."

Margaret digressed from our conversation, commenting that my Brooks Brothers suit would fit right in and that my colorful tie was a distinctive accessory. I thought this would be an appropriate time to begin wrapping up our meeting. Margaret had been more than generous with her time and information. I was getting a sense of how well Jerry's questions worked, and I now had a good picture of what it took for Margaret to be successful as a total quality manager. During my next networking interview, I planned to ask Jerry's question again.

I reached into my pocket for a small notepad, and in closing said, "Forty-five minutes is about up. Thank you. I greatly appreciate your spending this time and all the information you gave me. Before I leave, would you mind referring me to another of your colleagues or associates? I'm also open to looking at different industries."

On the ride home, I reviewed this informational interview. I was proud of the fact that I was patient and had concentrated on information gathering. As the job market had become more competitive, I'd been hearing others complain that many company contacts were refusing to grant informational interviews. Partially, that was because job seekers had become more manipulative, asking for one thing but doing the other. I thought a good motto for us job seekers would be:

Do what you say—
Informational interviewing is for information gathering.

That evening we were invited to dinner by Mike Fielder, my buddy from Technology, Inc. Mike walked in with a limp. He didn't talk about it much, but he had been hit by a piece of shrapnel in Vietnam.

"What can I get you to drink?" Mike said.

"A beer, thanks." When it came, I took a swallow. "Ah, the first mouthful always tastes so good," I commented. Then I looked around and said, "So Mike, have you done any looking outside of Technology?"

"In fact, I have. I had two interviews at a high-tech firm down the street from Technology."

"For what kind of position?"

"Oh, it was for a divisional production manager position similar to the one I have now, but the company in general seems more progressive than Technology."

"You don't seem very interested."

"No, I guess I'm not. The situation is too much like what I've been doing for the past six years. Besides I was told that they were interviewing about twenty experienced managers, all coming out of the high-tech industry. Out of the twenty, three would be selected for further interviews. I haven't heard anything in over a month, and I'm not interested enough to pursue it. There's a lot of competition out there."

"There sure is, Mike. Besides," I continued, "It sounds like you don't want to be doing the same old thing. You need some time to explore and think. I'm finding that my ability to make informed decisions is directly proportionate to the effort I put into asking questions and analyzing the feedback. If I'm clear about my own needs and what the job market has to offer, then I feel the power to go after opportunities."

"That's good common sense and hard work. So, Matt, if you don't mind my asking, how goes your job search?"

"Well, I'm making some progress. I'm becoming more clear about my job objective. As I network and do research, I'm leaning toward an internal organizational consulting position."

Lynda looked at Mike, then said pointedly, "I wish he'd hurry up and decide."

Suddenly, the atmosphere in the room felt tense. Mike said, "I'm sure Matt is doing all he can."

As I clutched my beer, Mike looked at us both and said diplomatically, "Let me know if I can help in any way. How about some hors d'oeuvres?"

On our drive home, I said, "Lynda, I wish you wouldn't chip away at me like that."

"Like what?" she snapped.

"Like when you interrupted my conversation with Mike. You said you wished I'd hurry up and decide. You know I'm doing my best. I thought we agreed I needed to take things step by step."

"You're being overly sensitive."

"I'm not," I snapped back. "You don't understand. I'm hurt. Thanks for the support," I retorted sarcastically.

"I can't always be supportive," shouted Lynda. "Why don't you work on keeping a little sense of humor?!"

We were silent for the rest of the drive home. This career transition was often painfully confusing and difficult. At times, I had difficulty discerning whether I was indeed overly sensitive. Also, Lynda's remark about humor rang a bell. I tend to get very serious — I usually call it focused — about things. Lynda's reaction indicated that my serious focus was affecting her life as well. Things built up for her; she didn't always tell me when she was feeling down or aggravated. Often I couldn't predict when or if we were going to hit one of these snags.

I'd learned when we'd gotten to one of our boiling points to temporarily drop the issue. After one of these episodes, I'd vacillate between anger and feeling rejected and lonely. Sometimes, I'd go for a walk, or I'd write in my journal. Later, after cooling down and thinking it over, we'd do better at discussing these matters.

As the weeks went on, I networked diligently, concentrating on continuous improvement. The philosophy of Margaret's company CEO was sound. After every interview I'd examine my behavior and look for ways I could improve, such as truly listening while the other person was talking rather than thinking about what I'd say next. My self-confidence was improving in response to the positive feedback I was receiving and the many referrals I was getting. Without prompting, people frequently would comment, "You're a natural when it comes to the business of quality management and consultation."

May 24

Back in February and March, I feared the unknown. Looking for a job seemed like an insurmountable task. I was afraid of what I had not tried. I felt injured, forced to change. Today, even without a job, I feel safer and less fearful. I am gaining a sense of purpose and direction. I've been dealing with my feelings by knowing that they do not go away over night, but that they can be talked about and managed. Also I'm assessing my skills, prioritizing my wants, and exploring organizations.

A recent Fortune *article noted: "Being laid off is never going to be an easy experience, no matter how common it becomes. The secret is remembering that, done right, it can represent an opportunity for greater self-knowledge, heightened self-fulfillment, and ultimately a better career."*

With practice, taking things step by step is becoming more automatic. I am pausing, taking deep breaths, and evaluating before and after I take action, take a risk. Gradually, I am converting my fear into positive change and opportunity.

I was looking forward to having the support group meet at my house and to discussing my next step—job interviewing. Lynda greeted Frank, the first member to arrive, on her way out to visit her sister. Betty and Jackie walked in as Lynda pulled out of the drive. It was a warm evening, so we met in the screened-in porch. I offered cranberry juice, coke, or water; then we got down to business.

Frank seemed anxious to present his issues first. He had a background in computer-aided design and also in architectural planning. Frank's goal was to combine his backgrounds to consult with architects on the use of state-of-the-art computer-aided design for their practices. "I don't know how to market my business," he exclaimed. "Furthermore, I've *never* had to sell. I used to do planning, program development, and design. Someone else sold. I need help."

Betty spoke first. "Selling is about building relationships," she said. "To build relationships, you've got to be able to listen, be patient, be competent in your field, and have faith."

Jackie added, "Also, it takes guts to get out there and put yourself in front of customers. To get going, you'll probably walk, and sometimes stumble, before you run. I've owned my own business, so I know."

I said, "Frank, I suggest you begin by networking. Discuss your business idea first with people you already know."

Frank listened attentively, then asked Jackie, "What do you think of beginning the sales process by networking?"

"That's how I began," she said.

I thought for a moment about my networking experience. The facts alone never got me in the door or generated helpful feedback. When the interviewer *felt* good about me, then the door *really* opened. Giving voice to my thoughts, I blurted out, "Frank, through networking you'll build relationships and *earn the right* to sell. Relationship building is the key, and sticking with that process will earn you the right." It was good to hear myself say these things. I'd lived them and believed in them.

It was already 8:35. My turn was last. I said to the group, "I want to begin job interviewing and am not sure where to begin. I've been successfully networking and am fairly clear about my vision. Basically, my goal is a management or internal consultant position in the area of total quality management in an organization that values individual and organizational learning."

Betty raised one eyebrow. "Boy, you are clear! Why don't you call back some of your network contacts to tell them you're now looking for a job?"

Frank piped up, "You've earned the right!" Betty was correct. I had the relationships, and Frank confirmed it. I had earned the right.

Betty continued, "One method I've been using as a networking tool is called a 'Networking Referral Sheet.' It saves me time, lets others know what I'm looking for, and gives them an easy and comfortable way to send information back to me."

"Please tell us more." Frank responded.

"Sure, but before I do, I've brought some copies for all of you. Included is a letter that tells my network contacts why I'm writing to them. The referral sheet has two essential parts: one is an explanation of what I'm looking for, and the other is a fill-in-the-blank section asking for specific contact information. Matt, you look as though you have a question."

"Yes. How do you get people to send these things back to you?"

"I make sure to include a self-addressed stamped envelope."

"So you're basically sending out three pieces in every package—an introductory letter, the networking referral sheet, and your self-addressed envelope."

Frank commented, "That sounds like a lot of work."

"It can be," responded Betty. "But I've learned to work smart. I've gotten results. I carefully select who my audience will be, and I mail not more than twenty at a time. My target audience includes people I've done business with, some of my former colleagues, and old college friends who are living in different parts of the country. Also, as I've expanded my network, I've asked new contacts if I could send them this information as a reminder—you know, just in case they come across something.

Networking Referral Sheet

Name: _____   Send-out date: _____

I am looking for: *people to contact who work for smaller*

companies (less than 1,000 employees) who may be aware

of jobs in financial planning.

The person you would recommend I contact is:

Name: _____   Phone number: _____

Company: _____   Title: _____

Street address: _____

City: _____   State: _____   Zip: _____

Date: _____   Referral source: _____

Other information about this person and/or company:

_____

_____

May I use your name?   ( ) yes   ( ) no

Thank you

This method works best in conjunction with phone networking, researching companies, and meeting new people. My mailing is working for me while I'm doing other things."

Frank nodded and said, "So I could try your networking method to drum up sales leads."

"That's right. I'm sure you could."

At 8:55, we all instinctively sat forward in our chairs. For a moment, I thought about the Celtics. Often without any apparent clue, the teammates align themselves for the next shot. As a group, we seemed to have some of this synergy. We were helping one another, and we seemed synchronized without effort.

Gateways

Do's and Don'ts

DO . . .

• Network; meet with others to gather information.

• Try different networking methods.

• Always write a thank-you note after a networking meeting.

• Ask others for their ideas about how to network successfully.

• Continue to sort out and express your feelings.

• Clarify the most important characteristics of a job that would interest you now (refer to the inverted doughnut).

• Join or develop a leaderless support group.

• Step back to evaluate your progress.

• Stay open to surprises!

DON'T . . .

• Confuse networking with job interviewing.

• Give up trying to reach someone. Try another way, another time.

• Discount how you've changed.

On leaving, Frank opened his car door, turned, and called, "See you next Tuesday night."

I responded with a big smile. "You bet. Jackie's at 7:30." As the last car pulled away, I stood waving at the end of our driveway. The darkness became the perfect background. There was the Big Dipper again, every star shining. I knew I was ready to go for it.

8

Starting Line

Express yourself

One of the books that George loaned me was *Transitions* by William Bridges.* I copied a couple of lines from the book onto the back of one of my old business cards.

> When we are ready to make a beginning, we will shortly find an opportunity. The transition process involves an inner realignment and a renewal of energy, both of which depend on immersion in the chaos.

This card had been in my wallet since mid April. As the end of May approached, I realized time had sped by. I had been immersed in the transition process. I was now clear about what I wanted, and I felt I was getting closer to an opportunity to take some action.

May 26

My severance runs out at the end of June. This scares me. But, I can't allow this fact to throw me off course. I've got savings and support from friends and family. Don't panic. *The way I manage my job campaign will be an outward expression of my "inner work."*
Stay on course.

*William Bridges, *Transitions: Making Sense of Life's Changes* (Reading, MA: Addison-Wesley, 1980).

During the past week, I had worked on my resumé. Some of my networking contacts and friends helped me with the fine-tuning and updating. I had decided to write a two-part resumé. The first page was basically a chronological synopsis of where I had worked and when. The subheadings of the first page included my objective, experience, education, and professional affiliations. Under experience, I placed the name of each employer, then the title of each job and a brief position description of each. I used my friend Maria's suggestion to place the dates of employment at the end of the last line of each position description. I had found this the most effective format when interviewing job applicants during my days as a manager. The dates of employment were not overly emphasized but were obvious enough and subtly informed the reader.

My objective read:

A consultant and/or management position with an organization that is utilizing total quality management as part of its strategic plan.

My objective spelled out the kind of position I was looking for, yet it was also broad. A variety of organizations—from high technology, to health care, to educational institutions—could have been appropriate as long as they had or were adopting total quality management.

The second page, titled "Capabilities and Accomplishments," was designed in a functional format. I divided the page into three parts that formed my "skill tripod." Total quality management, consulting, and leadership were the three functional legs that supported my objective.

Underneath each primary skill, I presented between three to five accomplishments. Every accomplishment was written as a clear statement, beginning with a verb. Each statement told what I did and with whom. Most ended with a result. Networking had taught me to design my resumé for a job market that was very result and solution oriented. An example of a statement that supported my expertise in TQM was:

Led three-day "Managing Quality Improvement" seminar for approximately sixty-five managers, resulting in increased understanding of TQM principles and written action plans to improve the development of teams.

Using a chronological plus functional two-page resumé would, I hoped, satisfy both the traditionalists and the more progressive employers.

I was learning to take pride in and ownership of every part of my job-search process. I made certain my resumé clearly demonstrated results, and I tailored cover letters to specific job requirements and organization needs. I intended to make sure each interview was an honest expression of me, and I would follow up with a thank-you note customized to the person and situation.

It was a cloudy Thursday morning, the first in the month of June. In about an hour I'd be meeting with John for my fourth session, my next to last. I quickly organized my desk and emptied the trash before I left. As the windshield wipers swept away the drizzle, I thought how the marketplace would be another testing ground for all my hard work and a reality check for my vision. The large striped tent and folding chairs set up for commencement as I drove by the community college reminded me that we would be attending Chris's graduation on Saturday. We were proud of Chris. Like our son, I was feeling optimistic about my future.

As I entered the office, John was saying good-bye to a stylishly dressed, striking, but sad-looking woman. I remembered those days. My tears didn't show on the outside, but they were certainly there on the inside. I thought, She's at the beginning; with John's help, she'll make it. "Welcome," said John, holding the door.

I paused for a moment, looked about, and sat in the chair crowned by Mozart's quotation, opposite the window. The gray light from the window fell on the Oriental rug at my feet.

"John, I'm ready to interview for jobs." I said. "In preparation, I've updated and rewritten my resumé. It includes a clearly defined objective, a chronological first page, and functional second page."

John nodded, then asked, "May I see a copy?" He looked it over silently, showing no signs of judgment. After three minutes or so, he simply beamed and asked, "May I use your resumé as an example for others?"

"Your request is a compliment. I'm flattered. Of course. Share my resumé with anyone you feel it would help."

"Thank you. Have you sent it to anyone yet?"

"No, I haven't. Ah, I think I've been waiting for your approval."

"You've got it."

"John, I wanted to mention my 'inverted doughnut.' I think it's an important part of lattice working."

"How so?"

"Well, as you can see by my drawing, there's substantially more 'space' than 'core.' When I thought about the work I enjoyed most, it involved projects that I initiated—ones that required my creativity, flexibility, and ability to plan and lead others. I'd say about one-third of a job like this would consist of a core—the defined job description. You know, like who I report to, budget deadlines, and reports that need to be completed."

"How will you use this information?"

"Mmm, I'm more clear about the job characteristics that are important for me to thrive. With this clarity I'll be better able to talk about and recognize a natural fit."

"Matt, I think you're right."

We talked about companies that I had visited while networking or had heard about that had adopted a TQM process. I had a couple in mind. Also, I'd go back to my personal Rolodex list to look for contacts who might refer me to other smaller companies. The two companies I intended to contact had fewer than two thousand employees, so I planned to address my cover letter and resumé to the presidents of each company.

"You've been effectively networking by asking questions and getting invaluable information," John commented. "For a moment, let's define job interviewing, then compare this activity to networking." I took some notes while John explained. "Interviews that work best are two-way conversations in which both parties feel as though they are winning. Winning does not necessarily mean that you get offered the job on the spot; this rarely happens. Success here means that you are able to sense the chemistry between yourself and the interviewer. It also means that you find out some specifics about the job, about the culture of the company, and some of the organization's expectations of people who work at your level." I smiled. I'd had this experience.

Matthew Townden
5 Unity Street
Lexingdale, MA 02110
(617) 841-2231

OBJECTIVE
A consultant and/or management position with an organization that is utilizing total quality management as part of its strategic plan.

EXPERIENCE
Technology, Inc. Manufactures computers and systems for process management and control.
Manager, Manufacturing Division
Managed a division of two hundred employees. Participated in the start-up and implementation of quality improvement teams. Developed inventory controls. Consulted divisionally. (1985-1991)

Mcom, Inc. Manufactures high-performance minicomputers.
Internal Senior Consultant
Designed work flow procedures for manufacturing. Delivered management training company-wide. Led a team in new product development. (1981-1985)

General Data, Inc. Develops data communications software.
Manager, Planning and Development
Managed staff of ten, achieving progressive alignment with strategic plan. Developed and implemented a companywide staffing plan. (1974-1981)

Electric Logic, Inc. Manufactures data acquisition electronic components and systems.
Manager, Manufacturing Systems
Developed and installed companywide manufacturing methods and systems. Reduced inspection requirements by 40% through introducing improved auditing methods. (1970-1974)

Breler Manufacturing Company, Privately held firm. Manufacturers digital/analog electronics.
Assistant Manager
Oriented new employees and developed the orientation program. Screened and interviewed potential hires. Assisted the manager in systems control and quality assurance. (1967-1970)

EDUCATION
M.A. degree in Business Administration
Boston University

B.S. degree in Education and Psychology
Boston College

PROFESSIONAL AFFILIATIONS
American Society for Quality Control
American Society for Training and Development

CAPABILITIES AND ACCOMPLISHMENTS

TOTAL QUALITY MANAGEMENT • Quality Certified • Leadership Awareness • Team Facilitator

Certified team leader and facilitator by Quality Associates, Inc., in their quality improvement process.

Planned and presented employee awareness programs. Achieved positive responses and interest; successful formation and start-up of nine quality improvement teams, one corporate task team, and one divisional lead team.

Guided vice president in charge of technology and facilitated his staff in planning and implementation. Achieved focused management participation, support, and continuity of work teams.

Led three-day "Managing Quality Improvement" seminar for approximately sixty-five managers and supervisors, resulting in increased understanding of TQM principles and written action plans to improve the development of teams.

Coauthored "Customers First" awareness workshop introduced in spring of 1990.

CONSULTING • Management/Supervisory • Goal Setting • Performance Management

Designed and conducted development surveys and needs assessments. Developed customized programs internationally, with management involvement and follow-through, for performance management systems, goals setting, and team building.

Initiated development of divisional quality assurance and JIT manuals. Resulted in ongoing divisional training in quality methods for employees and managers.

Developed and completed organizational effectiveness studies. Recommendations approved and implemented by senior management included changing reward systems, restructuring R & D to matrix teams, improving performance appraisal procedures, communicating performance expectations and goals, removing communication barriers.

LEADERSHIP • Succession Planning • Individual Development • Pioneering

Led and coordinated management succession planning effort. Identified high-potential replacement candidates. Results included performance criteria for the selection of successors, written competency profiles, individual development action plans, and filling critical positions with insiders.

Supported individual development programs with positive outcomes; specifically, retention of valued employees, alignment of personal and organization goals, improved performance communications, development plans and career pathing.

Pioneered and led manufacturing division in the development of a mission statement. Resulted in collective clarity of purpose and adoption of some of the same principles in companywide mission statement.

John continued, "An effective interview is a chance to express some of your accomplishments, discover what some of the organization's needs are, and share some solution-based ideas that could be relevant to the organization's concerns."

I stopped writing, and looked at John. "So you're saying a winning interview is a synapse between my beliefs and abilities and the organization's culture, product or service, and needs."

"Yes, that's a good way to think of it."

John believed my challenge would be to express my accomplishments in a manner that would be relevant to the organization's needs. I had become more comfortable and quite competent at questioning while networking. I figured I could attempt this challenge. Most of the time, striking a balance between making statements about myself and asking questions of the interviewer would work best.

John had a name for making a small change that would net big results; he called it "trimtab." A trimtab is a miniflipper attached vertically to the stern of the rudder of a boat. When the trimtab is maneuvered even slightly, it will change the course of the boat. John had a very good point. Interviewing would become less overwhelming and more manageable if I could identify small levers that would help facilitate bigger results. An example would be to determine at what point in an interview it would be appropriate to give specific examples of my ability to manage or consult and then give them.

Our time was about up. John said, "I'd like to end this session with a few more thoughts. First, the more competitive the job market, the more precious each interview becomes. You can't afford to be ill prepared. Also, Matt, you know yourself well and have clearly identified your skills. Interviewing that lands you a job will take practice. You'll be asked to tell your story to an audience that will judge you."

John stood up, wished me well, and handed me two Xeroxed sheets.

I turned to walk out, then pivoted back. "John," I said, "I've been here four times, and the scene through the window has changed every time. I realize I've changed continuously, too. Thank you." John nodded and gave me his knowing smile.

Trimtab

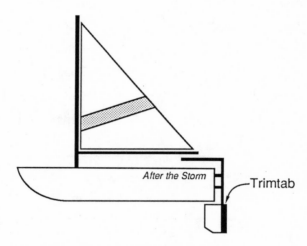

After the Storm
—Trimtab

A small change can shift your direction.

Examples:

1. Describe yourself in terms of your skills, not your title.

2. Ask a friend for a networking lead.

3. Dress up when making calls. Wear your business outfit.

4. Volunteer to help someone else.

List the small changes you can make:

1. _____

2. _____

3. _____

Interviewing Is a Balancing Act

Your unique needs	Organization's culture
Personality traits	Competencies
Preparation	Opportunity
Listening	Talking
Giving information	Getting information
Results you create	Team accomplishments

Balance between

For the past month, now that I was more clear about my direction, I had gone back to clipping job ads out of two or three papers. Three of the ads I'd clipped interested me. One was for an outplacement consultant, another for a TQM manager in a smaller high-tech company, and the third for a vice president of total quality management in a financial institution. That afternoon the sun began to shine, so I set up the card table on the screened porch. Until Lynda arrived, I wrote cover letters geared to each ad.

I had learned to reward myself in little ways, like sitting out on the porch while I wrote or taking a break to read *Sports Illustrated.* In our last group meeting, Betty had talked about feeling deprived and frustrated because the rewards she derived from interviewing were so unpredictable and intermittent. Jackie had responded by saying, "Have you considered a balance between short- and long-term rewards? For example, after I make five calls to set up interviews, I pick up my mystery novel and read ten pages. Also, after reading the financial reports of four *Fortune* 500 companies, I sit back and call a friend." As I dealt with my own chaos, some of my favorite rewards became renting a video and going to a ball game when the Sox were in town.

In Julia's workshop she had said, "Remember this acronym— TAP. TAP stands for Task, Action, Payoff." I learned to iden- tify a task (such as networking), follow through with action (such as calling five colleagues for contacts), then reward myself with a payoff (such as a walk).

Things seemed to be going pretty well. I was making progress, resolving my feelings, networking, building my confidence, and getting ready to interview. The phone rang. It was Eric, my man- agement consultant friend.

"Matt, I need to talk."

"Sure, what's up?"

"I never mentioned it, but the firm I've been working with has been having some hard times. The old story—revenues have been down, and overhead's been high. About five years ago, we located downtown, in one of those fancy office buildings. Back then, customers and money were flowing like the Mississippi. We still have some loyal customers, but we haven't been able to build new clientele fast enough. You know, to pay the lease and all."

"Mmm."

"This is the tough part. I was given notice."

"Notice?"

"I'm laid off. But not right away! I've got about three months to finish some client work; beyond that they gave me a couple months' severance."

As though it had never left, I felt that leaden feeling in my stomach. "Did you try negotiating for more?"

"I did. Initially, the president offered a one-month severance. He said, given the circumstances, he was doing his best. All of a sudden, I felt myself getting angry. I knew that was my sign that I was being treated unfairly. So I counteroffered and asked for another month."

"Sounds like he was pretty adamant. What reason did you give him?"

"My justification was that I agreed to stay on for as long as he needed to complete any work I had started. I reminded him how essential this was to client relations. I left it at that, and he agreed."

"You've got guts. Sorry to hear this is happening to you, too. You've been there for barely three years."

TAP: Task–Action–Payoff

Date: _____

Task: A specific job I need to do.
In this space write your task.

Action: What I'll do to get what I want.
In this space write the action step(s) that will lead to success in the task you stated above.

Payoff: The way(s) I'll reward myself for taking action.
In this space write how you will give to yourself for having taken action.

"Yeah, I know. When I think back, some of the signs were there, but you know how it is; I ignored them."

"Easy to do."

"Well, given that I still have a three-month window, I've decided to follow your lead."

"What's that?"

"Story telling. I decided I'd begin figuring out my story as to why I'm being let go."

"You mean before you actually leave?"

"Right. I've been denying the inevitable to this point. If I start telling my story now, by the time I actually leave, I figure I'll be in better shape."

"Mmmm . . . You've got a point. Besides, if you're clear about what you want, you could also start looking for a job. How can I help?"

"I'd like to drop by as soon as possible and show you some of the thoughts I've written down about leaving. Also, as I learned from you, I think it would be helpful to practice *telling* my story."

"I'm flattered that you've asked, and I'm happy to return the favor. Come over tonight, about 7:30."

That evening as we met, Eric decided he would ask the president to validate his "reasons for leaving." Given the increased caution of employers now, agreement on these reasons would act as a guideline, ensuring a congruent story should any potential employer ask for a recommendation. Eric reminded me that there was another reason for going through this exercise. It would eliminate some of his confusion and boost his self-confidence as well. To this end, we carefully crafted three reasons that were clear and honest and fairly represented Eric *and* his employer. After testing these reasons confidentially with a couple of his close colleagues, Eric presented them to the president for his comments and approval.

Eric boiled down his reasons for leaving Management Strategies, Inc., as follows:

1. During the three years Eric has been with Management Strategies, the company's needs have changed. At the time he came on board, the company's needs were for a senior management con-

sultant to set up, implement, and manage all aspects of management consulting.

2. As a result of these changes, Management Strategies will replace this function with a senior account representative. The focus will be on new client development. Although Eric has some ability in the sales area, it is not his primary talent or interest. We would like to see him use his strengths and interests.

3. These factors led to the conclusion that there was a mismatch of Eric's talents and the current needs of this company. Additionally, the company cannot carry the overhead of two positions.

The next morning, my responses to the three ads were in the mail, including resumé and cover letters. The TQM consultant ad asked for "a chronological salary history" as well. Instead, I decided to indicate my past salary range: $55,000 to $65,000. I hoped this would give them enough salary information, along with my other credentials, to initiate a first interview.

After assessing our financial obligations and budget, Lynda and I had determined that $50,000 was the least I could accept for a full-time position. For now, this amount, along with her salary, would be adequate. We felt setting a limit based on real information, as opposed to letting my ego needs get in the way, would help me clarify my priorities when job searching and give me more confidence during an interview. If a job met most of my criteria, taking a lower salary, within limits, was a worthwhile trade-off. I didn't want to raise any unnecessary red flags in an interview situation. Instead, I'd be clear about my limits and demonstrate my flexibility and clarity.

Through the grapevine, I had heard about Rita, a search consultant ("headhunter") who specialized in human resources and TQM recruitment. I had also heard about Rita via Maria, my human resource manager friend. As I ran along the path that morning, I debated whether to call Rita. My inner voice said, "Stay open. Stay flexible." My experience with headhunters had not been great, but she had a good reputation.

Rita sounded pleased, yet reserved, when I complimented her

about her fine reputation. I briefly shared my background with her. "You've had some terrific experience, and you sound upbeat," Rita responded. "I'd like to meet you this afternoon if possible. But I must warn you — the market is extremely competitive, unpredictable, and cautious. Yesterday a verbal offer was extended to someone I've been working with on a job search that began three months ago. This morning that requisition was pulled. So the candidate didn't receive a written offer."

"Rita, I guess this is a market where you can't take things too personally," I said. "And you don't have the job until the offer is in hand."

"Right, that's it!" said Rita. We agreed to meet at three that afternoon. Still, I was skeptical. How many people get jobs through recruiters? The statistics say not many. But my inner voice insisted, "Stay open. Stay flexible."

I had scarcely put down the phone when another call came in. When I answered, the caller said, "Jerry Brine here. Matt, how are you?"

"Good to hear from you. I'm fine. How are you?"

"Listen, Matt, I don't have much time. I've arranged an interview for you."

"With whom?" I asked.

"It's with Jim Kelly, one of my associates at the National Bank downtown, for an internal TQM consultant position. Just call to set up a time."

"Great. Thank you. I'll call."

After we hung up, I made a note on a yellow post-it to write Jerry a thank-you note. Networking, I thought, is paying off.

I headed straight for my car keys. Mrs. Lingren was going to spend ten minutes with me at eleven o'clock to review some interviewing material that the library was handing out as a service to the community.

As I walked in, Mrs. Lingren looked up and greeted me with her friendly smile. She handed me three information sheets: the first was the "Ten Commandments for Winning Interviews," the second was on preparation for interviewing, and the last was titled "Interview Strategy."

Ten Commandments for Winning Interviews

1. Know your past achievements. An achievement is something that excited you, gave you a feeling of pride, something that you enjoyed doing. Each achievement is made up of factors that have made you successful: creativity, for example, or management, directing, leading, or selling. Your core skills can be found by writing stories about your successes. Then, by underlining the qualities you've used to achieve and noting those used most frequently, your core skills will emerge.

2. Do your research. Gather and analyze information about the company and the companies' competition. Your painstaking research should include: what the company produces, who the company's customers are, what their culture is like, and if they have a company mission and, if so, what it is. Also find out if they are growing and why, what their plans are for the future, and who their primary competition is. Your knowledge about them will not only contribute to your self-confidence, but also show that you have sincere interest in them.

3. Answer all questions directly. Don't get long winded or go off on unrelated tangents. The best insurance for a direct response is *to listen: do your company research; and know your skills, achievements, values, and personal qualities.* Listening and preparation are the keys to a winning presentation at an interview. Decision makers are busy; they don't have time to listen to you ramble. This is an opportunity for you to demonstrate your effective, practical, and solution-oriented work style.

4. Be prepared to answer personal questions. Your personality and core values are strongly considered in a competitive market. Every person counts. You will not only contribute to the profitability of the company but also to its culture. You may be asked "What are your shortcomings?" "What is it about yourself that might offend someone?" "Describe the best or worst boss you ever worked for." "What do you want to contribute to this organization?" "What are your three top values?"

5. Balance listening with telling your story. Do not interrupt and sit back (don't slouch) when the interviewer is talking. Be brief when it's your turn to tell your story or answer a question. Pause and check in by asking "Would you like me to continue?" or "Am I answering your question?" or "Is there any aspect of my background that is of most interest?"

Ten Commandments for Winning Interviews (*continued*)

6. Focus on what you can do for them. Employers are interested in how you can solve their problems and work with their customers. Do not operate out of a "job description mentality" that emphasizes title, position, and narrowly defined responsibilities. Today, businesses are focusing on the customer. They look for people whose primary concern is the customer and the company and who want to roll up their sleeves and get to work.

7. Let the employer raise the issue of compensation. Remember this golden rule: If you bring up money first, you lose. All employers want to hire the best person for the job, especially in a competitive marketplace. They'll make you an offer if you've done your homework and have shown them the relevancy of your experience and ability to their needs. If they ask "What would you like?" respond, "I'd like you to make me an offer." Then you'll have additional significant information from which to think over their proposal and to counteroffer and negotiate.

8. Be bold—state your interest and why. In a competitive business market, employers hire people who know what they want and why. Often interviewers will not be as prepared as you are. So do your personal and company research. If the company and the specific job interest you, say so and why. For example, the organization may have similar values to yours regarding their respect for employee growth and development, or their product/service could contribute to the environment in a way in which you believe.

9. Relate your past experience to their needs. Hearsay is that all employers are looking for employees with experience in their specific industry—baloney! *Be prepared to demonstrate how your experience and skills are allied with their needs.* For example, tell a story about how you consistently met customers' needs. Also give examples of your fair and productive management style. Excellence in customer service and management is highly transferable if you can clearly demonstrate how.

10. Expand your options. Set up as many interviews as possible even when you think you have a hot prospect. You don't have the job until you've signed the acceptance letter. The job market is unpredictable: an employer with whom you think a job offer is imminent could lose a contract or could "surface" an internal candidate, both of which would adversely affect your candidacy. Also, you will be a much stronger negotiator if you know the market and have other active possibilities.

Interview Preparation

A simple way of identifying your skills and the proof of them before an interview is to tell a colleague or friend a story about one of your accomplishments. The story should consist of a beginning (what happened at the start), a middle (what you did), and an end (your accomplishment). Ask your colleague to write down skills and action phrases as you tell your story. During the next week or two, practice by telling several stories. Collect these stories in a folder for easy access so that you can examine your skills and accomplishments for interview preparation and confidence building.

Interview Strategy

First and foremost, skilled job seekers with excellent interviewing skills get jobs in any job market. So practice before you go for the bull's eye. If you've been networking diligently, you'll uncover companies and jobs that fit into three categories:

1. Most appealing (green zone)

2. Somewhat interesting (yellow zone)

3. Marginal (red zone)

Begin interviewing with red-zone companies for practice, then continue rehearsing with yellow-zone companies. By the time you've got to the green zone, you'll hit the bull's eye. The green zone represents the accumulation of your company research, self-knowledge, and abilities plus your dynamic interviewing skills. As fate often has it, a situation in the yellow zone could become a green-zone favorite. Stay flexible!

Mrs. Lingren knew me better than I thought. This information was right on target. As I drove home, I thought about using my twenty minutes at group the following Tuesday to rehearse interviewing. The idea of arranging companies and jobs so that they fit into three categories (green, yellow, and red zones) made good sense. This prioritizing method would help me focus and spread out some of the pressure that goes along with job interviewing. Also, if I were more interested in one job and/or company than another, I wanted to be able to practice on the situations I cared less about.

At 2:30, dressed in a light-weight dark gray suit and colorful tie, I slowly drove through the infamous five-way intersection. Just when I thought all was going smoothly, the red flashers signaled "Stop" on the school bus ahead. I turned the air conditioner on low and tapped my fingers to the mellow sounds of George Benson. I couldn't be late for my first meeting with Rita! Just before three o'clock, I took a sharp right into a small office park. There was the sign for her office, American Recruitment Services.

As I approached the second-floor entrance, I noticed my right hand was sweating from clutching my briefcase and from nervousness. Before I grasped the doorhandle, I switched the briefcase to my left hand and wiped my right hand on the inside of my pants pocket.

The receptionist's friendly manner suggested that she had greeted many professional types like me. She picked up the phone and told Rita that I had arrived. It has been almost four months since I'd been laid off, and it felt good to be taking action now. Looking back, I could appreciate the importance of taking some time to heal and to know myself better. I wondered what Rita would have to offer. Maybe she would be different from some of the other recruiters I'd met.

"Rita will see you now," the receptionist announced. My palm had stopped sweating.

Rita greeted me with a firm handshake. "Good to meet you, Matt," she said. We got right down to business. She didn't ask for my resumé right away but instead said, "We'll meet for approximately one hour."

"That should give us enough time." I felt confident, so I held out my resumé toward Rita. "Would you like my resumé?"

Her approach was different. She said, "Thank you for offering, but not right now. I'll look at it later. Right now I want to focus on talking with you."

I was a little puzzled, but before I could put the resumé back in my briefcase Rita asked, "Why did you lose your job?"

"I was laid off. Technology, Inc., the company I was working for, was bought by another. Layoff was one of their methods for consolidating resources." Rita nodded. I continued, "I've spent about four months assessing my strengths and skills. And also clarifying my objective."

"Getting clear isn't so easy."

"No, it's not."

"Okay. On the phone you mentioned your background and experience in management and TQM consulting. Would you tell me about some of your experience in these areas?"

This was where my practice would pay off. I asked, "Rita, are you most interested in examples of my abilities in consulting, management, or leadership?"

"Start with leadership, why don't you."

I began, "As a leader I believe in setting an example for the whole division or organization. I don't expect others to do what I don't expect from myself. I figure I'll be learning how to be a leader all my life. My ability is reflected by the people that I'm leading."

I paused for a moment and continued, "I'm a leader who believes in cooperation and participation. I've learned you can't force change. Companies and people are too complex. My credibility has been gained through actions that produced results. The size of the step forward was not as important as the movement forward. I rewarded people who produced results *and* participated." I glanced over at a poster on the wall that read "Job Number 1 Is Quality." As I turned toward Rita, I said, "Would you like me to be more specific about results?"

"Yes, Matt. But first, may I look at your resumé?" I reached over to the side table and handed Rita my two pages.

She scanned them quickly. She had probably seen hundreds of these. "Good job," she said, looking directly at me. "I like the combination of the chronological and functional formats. No need to go into results, Matt. You've got many clear examples right here."

Rita was representing her corporate clients by screening for individuals who matched the organizational culture and who had produced results. These results had to be examples of productivity that related to the current needs of the organizations (her customers). As her thorough manner suggested, she had built her reputation on producing good matches—another reminder that the marketplace was solution based and results oriented.

Rita shifted gears for a moment. "The marketplace is a tough one," she said, "but I think you're a strong contender." I thought, it sounds like I'm competing in some athletic event! "Matt," she added, "I'm glad we've met. I've got a couple of situations in mind. One in particular, at a medical facility, matches your criteria for a position in internal total quality consulting." She added, "On a practical note, the facility is about a half-hour commute from your home."

As we were getting up from our seats, Rita said, "I hope you don't mind this question; if you do, say so. Are you getting a severance?"

"That's a fair question. I've had a severance for four months. It's about up. I've also got some savings, and my wife works." I added, "Of course, I'd like to find the right job as soon as possible."

"I'm sure of that," Rita replied.

I realized that it would have been detrimental to project any kind of desperation concerning my finances, so when the issue was brought up, I gave a direct and positive answer.

I left Rita's office at about four with a renewed faith in recruiters. Rita had encouraged me to describe my ideal scenario; she was realistic, not discouraging. Her feedback about my resumé was, "Let's try this and see what results we get." And my intuition said she would follow through regarding the opportunity we discussed.

Rita certainly came across as a seasoned recruitment specialist. She had begun in her profession in the days when newspaper employment ads would specify "male or female." Clearly, she exuded business savvy and had a reputation as a matchmaker extraordinaire. Her approach was straightforward. She openly said, "I'm out to make a match that pleases employee and employer."

Setting up interviews in this market wasn't easy. On Monday

and Tuesday I logged forty-three calls. A record for me! In most instances, people were traveling, they didn't have jobs, the job was already filled, or they suggested I mail a resumé. It seemed that my best source of interviews was through my network. Following up Jerry's lead, I had scheduled to meet on Wednesday afternoon with Mr. Kelly, senior vice president of finance at the National Bank. Before then I would do some research on the company and then practice interviewing with my support group Tuesday evening.

On Tuesday afternoon I received a form letter from the personnel department of the high-tech company to which I had sent a resumé. It said they'd let me know if my credentials met the specifications of any of their future positions.

Forget home runs; getting on base was tough enough. Job searching took a lot of perseverance, patience, and planning. I'd learned to develop working plans that were flexible, were divided into steps, and had a purpose. Flexible planning allowed me to make alterations as I assessed myself and as circumstances changed in the marketplace. I'd sit down at the end of every day to review my course of events and then write my plan for the next day. This was my time to pat myself on the back for my accomplishments and to create realistic anticipation for the next day.

My means for coming up with job interviews included networking, classified ads, employment agencies, and faith. Back at Technology, we had used "scenario plans." Simply put, if one method didn't work, we'd use another. I wasn't going to put all my eggs in one basket. Whether I called it a flexible daily plan or a scenario plan, much of the process remained the same. Staying flexible, moving step by step, analyzing and learning, and replotting my route were integral elements.

Tuesday evening before the group meeting, I reviewed the job search calls I had made and decided which companies I'd send resumés and letters to. Lynda agreed to ask me some practice interview questions. Some of the questions I answered included: "Tell me about one of your most recent accomplishments with your past employer." "Why did you consider this an accomplishment?" and "Describe the kinds of people with whom you work the best." I did okay, but as Lynda pointed out, I had a tendency to ramble. Practice and feedback would help streamline my responses.

Wednesday morning I called back some of my network contacts for job leads and reread materials on the National Bank. That afternoon, walking into Mr. Kelly's office, I was impressed with its feeling of grandeur and permanence. The decor included intricately patterned wall-to-wall carpeting with just the right amount of cushioning. The maroon of the carpet matched the drapes and accented the soft patina on the red/brown mahogany walls. Mr. Kelly was a big man with a confident, ready smile. He sat on the sofa and graciously motioned for me to take a seat in the cushioned armchair.

"Call me Jim," Mr. Kelly began. Almost instantly, the formality of the office became less intimidating, balanced by Jim's friendly and casual style. He did not waste time. "The chairperson of our company doesn't believe in slogans like 'Do it right the first time,'" he said. "He believes effective management makes productive change. Slogans frustrate employees and misguide their best intentions."

I agreed. "Employees need ownership of the work process, training, and a fair reward system, not slogans." I paused and scanned the room, noticing that there was no desk. Instead, there was a tall lectern table with no chair.

"Here," Jim continued, "we believe in an eclectic quality approach. We use the methods developed by well-known quality experts such as Deming, Crosby, and Juran." The hour flew by as our conversation progressed toward direct applications of quality philosophy and methods. Jim slid his arm off the back of the sofa and sat forward. He said, "We have an internal quality consultant position available. If you are interested, call me next week. I like your style and experience."

As Jim walked me toward the door, I asked, "Where is your desk?"

"I haven't had one in years," he said. "I stand at that lectern to do my work. It keeps me alert and out of the office visiting the troops!" I thanked him and agreed to call the next week.

I was flattered by Jim's invitation, but I was also cautious. As though linked together in a chain, every sector—including retail, manufacturing, high-tech, and financial services—was influenced by these changed economic times. Predicting outcomes in this job market was a fool's game. At any point there could be a scandal uncovered in a bank, or the stock market could take a nose dive. I planned to do some further research on the financial condition of National Bank and, through my network, ask around about the experiences of people who had worked there.

My job interview strategy was to get five interviews going in, I hoped, different sectors for both management and consulting positions. At group the night before, Betty had said, "It's been tough getting even just one or two interviews that are relevant to my background." I needed to see if I could accomplish my goal.

The evening news was discouraging. Lynda and I looked at one another as the reporter announced, "Layoffs are cutting deeper into the ranks of white-collar workers." They interviewed a forty-eight-year-old laid-off general manager who questioned ever again working in his lifetime in a job that was challenging and paid at his level. "Food kitchens are busier than ever," the reporter continued, "with people in line who never imagined they'd be there." I looked at Lynda and said, "Thank God for food kitchens. I'm scared enough that I'm going to do my very best never to be there."

"Matt, I get scared, too. I hate to worry you, but I'm concerned about paying Chris's tuition. He deserves to go to grad school."

"I'm concerned, too, but I try not to focus on the negative. I promise you I won't let my search interfere with Chris's schooling."

Lynda turned off the television and said, "How will we pay his tuition if you're not working?"

"Let's see, I'd probably call Russ and ask his advice. If need be, we'd borrow the money. It would only be a temporary loan."

"From where? From whom?"

"First, I'd try a bank. Our credit has been good. If not that, I might ask my brother. We don't know yet; Chris may get a partial scholarship."

"Those are some options, you're right. Chris has also had an excellent year. Matt, I just had to bring this up. Let's not worry about it until we have to. Still, I think it's a good idea for us to talk about these issues."

Lynda started to get up, then sat down again leaning on the edge of the sofa. She added, "You know, I don't want to get like I was at Mike Fielder's party. I never apologized for that. I'm sorry."

I took Lynda's hand and said, "Thank you. I agree — it's better to talk about things as they come up. I think we're both getting better at that."

We hugged.

I felt sad on Thursday morning to think I'd be having my fifth and last session with John. This was another ending. I felt like I was saying "So long" to the guide who had helped me up the mountain. Oh, I did the work (step by step), but his encouragement and support had been invaluable.

John was so consistently upbeat and sincere. As usual, he held the door as I walked in and greeted me with his characteristic smile.

"John, I'd like this to be my last session," I began. "I feel that I've healed fairly well, and that I'm on my way. I don't expect job interviewing and getting the job I want to be easy, but I'm confident of my inner resources. Also, I'm going to keep going to my support group Tuesday evenings."

John was clearly not surprised. "You're a fast learner, you're motivated, and this world needs you," he said. "You'll do fine. Just let me know which lucky organization gets you!"

We spent the next forty minutes talking about values and about selling myself in the job market. John talked about some of his observations. "Matt," he said, "it seems that many people who have been laid off and are job searching like you are looking for avenues to fulfill their needs for inner meaning as well as other values." I nodded. John continued, "Getting paid well and giving to others, having power and empowering others, and achieving your goals and inspiring others do not have to be conflicting aims. By using the lattice approach — clarifying your values, listening, and speaking up for what you believe — you'll become attractive to those organizations that are looking for clear thinkers who can change things for the better."

"John," I said, "In this market my values are really being tested. Organizations are looking for people who can resolve these contradictions. During informational and job interviews, I listen for certain phrases: 'work as a team,' 'open communication,' 'sharing of ideas,' and 'respect for the customer.' I'd be interviewing with more companies if I weren't so particular about joining a company that believes in its employees."

John responded, "So you're saying *you also have the right to choose, even in this marketplace.*"

Without hesitating, I nodded and said, "Sure, after I've clarified what I want and how I'll add value to a company. Choosing, isn't that a cornerstone of the lattice approach?" I had decided I would hold out for my goal to the end. Compromising my values was out of the question. If need be, I would sell alarm systems as an interim job while I looked for a good job fit.

John smiled. "In our last fifteen minutes," he said, "let me make a couple of comments about selling." He went on, "Selling is when you test what you know. It is the process you engage in when interviewing for a job, arranging informational interviews, securing a loan for a small business, and convincing an employer to upgrade a position. This is when all your research and self-assessment pay off. Some of your sales tools for effective selling are your resumé, cover letters, presentation skills, and thank-you notes. To make a sale—land the job you want—you'll be continuously improving your skills in listening, questioning, expressing, intuiting, and creating."

John paused, and I questioned, "You didn't mention closing the sale."

"Yes, very astute of you," John commented. He excused himself for a moment, walked to his desk, and turned down the volume on his answering machine. He sat back down.

I blurted out, "So closing, or getting the job I want, is a *natural* outcome of being skilled at all the other tools?"

John smiled. "Remember, you can't control when the sale happens," he said, "but you can be the master of your own behavior throughout the process."

We both sat forward in our chairs. I said, "John, I believe my work with you has been about renewal. I was stagnating at Technology, Inc. Layoff was the push I needed to get me going. I agree with you—I've learned to take control of my career."

John stood up, took a step forward, shook my hand warmly, and said, "Working with you was a pleasure. Take care."

I could barely say, "I will." As I opened my car door, I thought, Here is another starting line. I have relied on John as my guide. The time has come to cut the cord and use my inner resources to navigate toward a meaningful job.

During the next two weeks, I set up three interviews. Rita had arranged for me to interview for a job as a senior quality consultant with a local hospital. Also, there was a message on my machine from a downtown outplacement firm; the director invited me to interview for a part-time consultant position. A local manufacturing organization had recently laid off about two thousand workers at all levels. The outplacement firm had already contracted with the manufacturer to counsel blue-collar employees. The firm was screening for consultants in anticipation of working with the executives as well. The message said: "Matt, this is Donald Spray of International Outplacement Group. I'm calling in regard to your unusual letter in response to my ad in the *Patriot Ledger* last Thursday. Please call me at your earliest convenience to see if we could set up a time to kick some things around. Thank you."

At the time, I didn't think my letter was so unusual. I decided not to send a resumé or an in-depth letter that outlined my qualifications, but only a brief, straightforward note. I needed to distinguish myself, to get on first base. I wrote:

June 15, 1992

Mr. Donald Spray
President
International Outplacement Group
P.O. Box 347
Boston, MA 02110

Dear Mr. Spray:

You undoubtedly will receive several resumés in response to your ad for outplacement consultants. I am a businessman and a seasoned, experienced manager who has coached several employees on career/job transition issues.

If you would like someone with a fresh perspective on outplacement counseling and are interested in implementing new systems and processes, I'm that person. I offer you and your clients integrity, common sense, and a vision for the future. If you are interested in meeting me, please call. I would be interested in meeting you.

Sincerely,

Matthew Townden

I figured if I were offered a part-time job, I could also continue my search for a management or TQM consultant position. Also, this outplacement position would be more than a way station. I could be a catalyst, as John was for me, to help others overcome their fears and learn tools for achieving their goals.

I knew I'd be good at this work, given my past experience in industry as a manager who had coached several employees plus my recent experience going through the layoff process. People who were laid off needed help from professionals who could identify with their situations. I could certainly identify and would be able to listen, guide, and encourage others.

The third interview was a result of my calling back Jim Kelly at the bank. Even though we had set up a further meeting, something puzzled me about Jim's response. I think it was the tone of reservation in his voice. After talking with a few former employees, my research about the bank had yielded a mixed review: there was some question as to the CEO's commitment to quality as well as a loss of the bank's market share to increased competition. I reserved judgment and thought I'd learn more in my second interview next Wednesday. These days many organizations were losing market share, and the quality process frequently slipped, especially at first, owing to poor leadership support and ambivalence about change.

On the positive side, the senior consultant position at the hospital sounded very appealing. Rita explained, "Matt, I've met the CEO and most of his staff. In a word, they struck me as enlightened. It seemed that they viewed quality as a process, not as a program—a process that empowers individuals and the organization toward identifying and addressing customers' needs."

I felt myself getting excited but tried to remain calm. "Rita," I said, "could you tell me something about the position itself?" I could feel her excitement as well. She had seen enough of these situations to know that this would be a good match with my background and personality.

She read the job description: "'The primary responsibility for this senior consultant is to lead the hospital in the achievement and maintenance of excellence in service delivery through the use of TQM methods and strategies.'" She went on, "You would lead the continuous quality improvement process by supporting and monitoring quality improvement action plans and facilitating focus groups. Also, you would provide coaching to work team facilitators." Rita continued to tell me about the skills and abilities required, some of the interpersonal requisites, and the working conditions. She had already set up an initial interview for next Friday morning for me to see the employment manager and the vice president of human resources.

"Thank you," I said. "I'm thrilled. I'll call beforehand if I have any questions. After the interview, I'll give you a call to tell you how things went. In the meantime, I'll do my research."

Soon it was into the fourth week of June. The three interviews seemed to happen in a burst. My support group had been helpful in encouraging me to continue networking for other job interviews. Even though my goal was to have at least five interviews going, it seemed more difficult to land two others, knowing that I had three already.

Or at least I thought I had three. On Wednesday morning, as I slipped my tie on for my second meeting with Jim at the bank, the phone rang. A youthful professional voice said, "Good morning. I'm calling from Mr. Kelly's office. There has been a change in plans. Mr. Kelly cannot meet with you this morning due to an executive committee meeting. He also asked me to say that he regrets that the job for an internal quality consultant has been put on hold. I'm sorry. Good luck looking for a job." Click!

My heart began to race. I hoped the other two interviews didn't fall through. I had no backups. I couldn't predict what was going to happen in this market. The reservation I had sensed in Jim's voice had meant something. And my severance pay and benefits were about to run out.

I went out to the screened porch and stood looking into the woods. Slowly I began to calm down. This is not a catastrophe. This type of thing happened to applicants frequently when I was working at Technology, Inc. I kept my tie on and wrote Jim Kelly a note thanking him for his honesty. I also expressed my hopes that things would improve at the bank. I didn't ask him to consider me again if they resurrected the position. I figured that was implied.

I spotted the note Chris had sent to me weeks earlier. I perked up when I read "Patience and perseverance." The rest of that morning I spent networking for job leads. Just before lunch I got a call from Jackie announcing that Betty had received a job offer as a financial planner in a small software company. I commented, "That's great! She deserves it. Isn't it encouraging to know that people are getting jobs? By the way, how did she find it?"

"Betty's ingenuity and networking paid off. One of the contacts that she sent her networking referral sheet to sent her back the name of a small company and its president. You know Betty; she did her research, then went after the opportunity. Betty's especially excited about her job because it's going to be a welcome change from working in a large company."

One member of our leaderless group had achieved her goal. We continued with three members. After seven group meetings, Frank had made many contacts and was trying to stay optimistic, given that he hadn't closed a sale yet. Jackie and I were still in the throes of interviewing and job networking.

Mr. Kelly had gotten back to Jerry to say that he was impressed by my experience as a manager and by my knowledge of TQM. On the other hand, he commented that my eye contact could have been better and that sometimes I appeared unnecessarily anxious.

This feedback was not easy to hear, although it was the experience of me of someone I respected. As I thought about it, it was true that occasionally I did get intimidated by some senior players. Also, being out of work had eroded my self-confidence. After all, they had something I didn't have — a job!

I decided to take a look at my interviewing skills by contracting with an outplacement consultant for a two-hour video and feedback session. As John had said, "The more competitive the job market, the more precious each interview becomes." I couldn't afford to be ill prepared.

The interview and feedback session with Ric, the outplacement consultant, was pretty straightforward. Ric interviewed me for three-quarters of an hour and played back the video. At particular points, I asked to stop the tape so that we could talk about my behavior. During other segments, Ric interjected his points of view.

I was already familiar with many of the questions he asked, such as "When were you laid off?" "Tell me about one of your most significant accomplishments," and "How do you feel about your past employer?" It was helpful seeing myself on film and getting professional feedback.

For example, when Ric asked, "How do you feel about your past employer?" my eye contact was almost nonexistent. I had looked over at a picture on the wall and answered, "They had to trim expenses. I was one of the first managers to be let go. I've heard through some of my colleagues that several other managers have been laid off since. I didn't take it personally." When Ric played back this segment, he said, "Matt, I see a discrepancy between your words and body language. You seemed uncomfortable and looked away when you answered."

I swallowed, then responded, "The video doesn't lie."

"Don't judge yourself. Instead, you've got something here you can work on and improve."

"But how?"

"Talk with friends and your wife about your feelings." He also asked, "Have you considered writing about your feelings?"

"Yes, I've been keeping a journal."

"Good. You've already got some practice. For a while focus on your writing on what Technology, Inc., meant to you. Write about what and who was positive. Also write about what stunk! This way you'll be able to see the differences more clearly."

"You mean I'll be able to separate my positive experiences from the negative?"

"Yes, exactly. In an interview you'll have more confidence. You'll be able to relax and talk about what was positive."

"I understand. I know that employers want to hire people who are positive and confident."

Just before I left, Ric explained, "I just want to add that continual eye contact isn't natural either. Looking away, down, or toward a corner momentarily is a way to give you and the interviewer a break. Also," he added, "if you get asked a tough question, say to the interviewer 'I'd like a moment to think about that.' Then pause and put your head down. As you begin to raise your head, say 'Now I'm ready,' then give your answer."

Starting Line
Do's and Don'ts

DO . . .

- Clarify your job objective.

- Reevaluate your finances.

- Combine chronological and functional formats when writing your resumé.

- Reward yourself; take pride and ownership in your efforts.

- Plan and take smaller risks; they'll add up to your bigger goals.

- Review and practice the "Ten Commandments of Winning Interviews."

- Expand on the ways you develop interviews—networking, classified ads, employment agencies, and calling companies directly.

- Act! *Focus* on today.

- Call members of your "leaderless group" for support.

- Continue to learn from your journey.

- Make a list of what was positive and what was not when working with your past employer.

DON'T . . .

- Panic if your severance runs out.

- Use a chronological resumé as your only marketing tool.

- Take uninformed, large risks.

- Let your anxiety drive you into taking any job.

- Judge yourself for learning and trying.

On the way out, I decided to put Ric on my board of Life, Inc. He'd been very helpful.

When I got home, I took out my journal and, following Ric's suggestion, wrote:

June 27

Thoughts regarding Technology, Inc.

What was positive?	*What stunk?*
• *Streamlining and building the manufacturing division*	• *Mr. Carroll's attitude and management style*
• *Implementing quality work teams*	• *Losing many hard-working employees to layoffs*
• *My buddy Mike Fielder*	• *Unqualified employees from the parent company edging out Technology, Inc., workers*
• *Leading and managing a group of great employees*	
• *Helping direct the growth from traditional management to TQM*	• *Feeling less effective—getting depressed*
	• *Loss of control after the merger/buyout*
• *Open communication between my employees and me*	• *Lack of trust in the new leadership of Technology, Inc.*
• *The career management classes I sponsored and attended before the merger*	• *Seeing programs my team and I put in place get scrapped indiscriminately*
• *Being pushed to try something else*	• *All succession planning and career development put on hold*
• *Experiencing a merger and corporate buyout*	• *Getting kicked out of my office and transferred to another*

9

Taking Chances

Everything to gain

The situation with the International Outplacement Group looked tentative. Part of the interview process included giving a presentation about how I would consult with someone who had just been laid off. I passed this one with flying colors! I was put on their list of part-time backup consultants should their corporate accounts warrant additional help. It seemed that in the past year or two, outplacement had become a viable profession in and of itself, what with the increase in company layoffs. The candidate pool was starting to get saturated. I became part of the backlog.

As I'd hoped, the most probable and exciting possibility was with the hospital as senior quality consultant. My first two interviews seemed right on target (in the green zone). They were back to back on July 10, one with Nancy Vilner, the employment manager, and the other with Carl Simms, the vice president of human resources.

Carl said, "Matt, some of our suppliers are late with their deliveries. For instance, Aide First, Inc., supplies us with brand-name bandages, dressings, and antiseptic applications. They are one of the best in the business, yet their deliveries are frequently late. Our doctors, nurses, and patients depend on them. How would you, as our internal quality expert, deal with this situation?"

"I'd like a moment to think," I said as I looked down. As I raised my head I replied, "It sounds like you'd prefer to retain Aide First. They provide the right products, of excellent quality, and at a competitive price, but their product delivery is unreliable."

"Right." Carl replied. "Our primary complaint is that doctors, nurses, and, most important, patients — our customers — can't depend on them for on-time delivery."

I then demonstrated how I could become part of the solution. "I'd call a meeting between the person in charge of inventory and deliveries at Aide First and the people here who represent the customers being affected by this service. At the meeting I'd present the issue. I'd be careful not to blame any one party; I'd simply raise the problem."

"No blame — that's a good point," commented Carl. "Go on."

"Then," I said, "I'd reinforce that we are looking for solutions. Also, I'd make the point that we have been receiving the right products, which are of excellent quality, at a competitive price. My goal would be to have us work together as a team to create a higher-quality service, meaning on-time delivery. I'd probe for what the members felt was getting in the way of 'total quality' customer satisfaction."

"Customer satisfaction is our aim," confirmed Carl.

"I take a systems view of these issues," I continued. "This means that all parties involved are interconnected. If I can get each member to own his or her part of the problem, then each one can contribute to the solution."

Carl was listening intently. I said, "Eventually, I would hold a meeting like this with each vendor and hospital group responsible for customer satisfaction."

"Your approach is thorough and respects all parties. I like that," said Carl. "In the end," he concluded, "everyone of us is responsible for ensuring quality."

My intuitition told me that this was a successful interview. I demonstrated how I could benefit the organization and add value to the customer. Today, most organizations are concerned with what value the job seeker will provide. Jumping on the band-

wagon or riding on someone else's coattails is no longer toler-
ated. Companies can't afford the baggage; it's not profitable.

What made this situation most difficult was, paradoxically,
what also made it potentially so wonderful — that it was a "natural
fit." I could not control the outcome. To ease my anxiety, I repeated to Lynda, Chris, and George, "It's a natural. It's a natural."
I was a little more restrained with Rita. She reminded me, "Stick
with the process, do your research, stay grounded, and don't
predict the outcome." I heeded her advice.

Finally, it was the end of July. We had been living off of Lynda's
income and our savings for one month. Up to this point, I hadn't
found another full-time position that interested me, despite my
diligent networking. "Lynda," I said, "even though we are fru-
gal, without my income, everyday expenses feel like sand swiftly
flowing through an hourglass." At this point, I was feeling torn
between temporarily working part-time or staying focused on
my professional job search. I grew even more anxious during the
first two weeks of August, when still neither Rita nor I had heard
from the hospital regarding my candidacy. We concluded that
they were interviewing other applicants. I also heard through the
grapevine that they had surfaced an internal candidate. In this
market, when it came to hiring, organizations were taking their
time and could afford to be very selective.

The last issue of the *National Business Employment Weekly* had
advertised a workshop titled "Focus — Get a Great Job in the
Smaller Business Market (SBM)." The introduction read, "Highly
interactive and creative workshop where participants will learn
the skills to develop job opportunities in the SBM. You may be
thinking 'Large companies have very few jobs and those that exist
don't interest me, so where and how do I look elsewhere? I've
worked for larger companies, what are some of the characteristics of smaller companies that I would need to know in order
to give me an edge in my search?'" The workshop ad quoted *USA
Today:* "As large companies continue to cut their middle-man-
agement ranks, most jobs will be created in small to mid-size companies employing 100 to 2,500 workers." I was sold. I had to
learn new methods that would increase my options in this hidden job market. Besides, all larger organizations began as part

of the smaller business market (SBM). I believed I could make a contribution to a smaller business success.

When I called the consulting firm to register, I asked if one of the consultants would elaborate on what I could expect to learn. I was informed that the primary objective of the workshop was to teach participants a "marketing letter approach" for finding a job in the SBM. He explained, "A marketing letter is not just a single document, but rather an approach. Like an iceberg, its tip — your letter — is merely a representation of its massive foundation. A marketing letter is a purposeful and well-researched document based on a foundation of prework. In your letter you are proposing that you could meet some of the needs of a particular organization based on your background and the extensive research you have done. Furthermore, your document states that you will be proactive. This means that you will call the employer to determine if it would be beneficial to schedule a meeting. And in the meeting you will discuss how your skills, experience, and abilities could be of value to them." One of the principles of the lattice approach, "do your outer work," also emphasized organizational research and discovering ways to benefit the company.

My daily runs, along with my individual and group support, helped keep me on course. This year, Lynda had to persuade me to go to our neighbor's Fourth of July party. I was feeling especially vulnerable, given the precarious state of my job search, and was reluctant to mix with others. As the night sky burst into a cascade of light and color and escalated into a chaotic grand finale, I thought about the beginning of my transition and my progress. The clouds of smoke were erased by a mild breeze, revealing my friend, the Big Dipper. My choice was clear, I thought, I was going on to my own grand finale.

During the last two weeks of August, I was called back to the hospital six times to interview with the CEO, with members of the executive committee, and with line managers. They examined my accomplishments, my approach to solving problems, the relevancy of my past business experience to their culture, and my values. Each meeting led to another and helped confirm my intuition that this job was a natural fit.

In the meantime, although my heart was set on the job with

the hospital, I attended the SBM workshop. To my surprise the majority of the participants had not been laid off but were professionals who were choosing to investigate other career options. For example, one of the members, a university professor, summarized why the majority was there when he said, "Even though I've been successful, I feel trapped, unchallenged, in a shell that no longer fits. My values have changed, and I need a new challenge. I'm here to discover how to get out and move on."

The workshop facilitator, Penny Foster, introduced herself in a thought-provoking manner. "During the past twenty years I have been an artist, art teacher, employee relations representative, and placement specialist. Now my job title is outplacement counselor/workshop facilitator. My 'career theme' has involved the *utilization of my creativity*. I've made all of my career experience count by moving in five different, yet connected, directions." She chuckled. "At this rate I've got at least five more moves!"

Seeing that everyone seemed curious, Penny continued, "I shared my background in this way to illustrate how you can take risks at any age and get what you want. I'm nearly fifty years old. As far as I can tell, my age has been an asset, coupled with my creativity and accumulated knowledge. These qualities count because I make them count. In essence, I get paid for them."

Craig, the young entrepreneur in our group, spoke up. "Can you tell us more about what you mean by career theme? I've just sold my dry cleaning business, and I'm wondering how knowing my career theme will help me answer what's next."

"A career theme is different than a career objective. Your career theme helps guide you toward your career objective—a statement about what you want to do. It is an expression, a word or phrase, of what you *truly* value—creativity, technical skills, independence, managing others, security, and so on. You can identify your career theme by becoming more conscious of the choices you've made throughout your career and why you've made them. It is also important to note your successes and to examine the skills that have played an important role in your achievements. Think of your career theme as a melody that's repeated—in the jobs you've had, in the projects you've completed, and in the other roles you've assumed professionally."

My journal, I thought, could aid in helping me identify my career theme. I'd take the time to reread some of my entries. Also, when I wrote, I'd focus more on *why* I made particular project and job choices.

For a minute or so the group seemed to be thinking. Craig jumped up and said, "I've got it! I'm one of those people who's been happiest doing a whole bunch of different things. When I owned the dry cleaners, I used to press shirts, keep the books, wait on the customers, negotiate with vendors, and manage my employees. I loved the challenge. Also, when I think back to working in my father's business, I used to test myself by doing all sorts of things. I took full advantage of the autonomy I had by involving myself in a variety of tasks that contributed to the business."

Penny asked, "Why did you sell a business you loved?"

"Well, I learned it wasn't the business that I loved, it was the variety of things I did to run it. Besides, when I got married last year, I thought I could work seven days a week *and* have a relationship. I learned otherwise."

Penny responded, "Bottom line, it sounds like you thrive on *variety* and *challenging* work. Don't simply buy my analysis. I'd like you to think about whether this is so. Craig, as we talk about the 'marketing letter approach,' you'll gain clarity and get some ideas as to where and how you can express your theme."

The "marketing letter approach" was based on this reality: the marketplace was saturated with resumés. As I learned in the beginning of my transition, a company can receive hundreds of resumés for one position. Penny called them "junk mail."

She continued, "I suggest an alternative to the resumé—that each of you use an expertly researched marketing letter that tells a company *how you can benefit them.* Every one of you, regardless of your goal, should think of yourselves in terms of being self-employed. If you're successfully self-employed, you've got to be constantly thinking of and acting in ways to contribute to the bottom line and add value to the customer. To make your case, you need to do research on the company—beforehand." Craig was nodding as Penny continued. "In today's job market the employer is the customer. The question for each of you is, What value can *you* add?"

During the rest of the afternoon, we struggled through the first draft of a marketing letter. With Penny's coaching, we tried to explicitly and succinctly state what we would bring and add to a potential employer. I addressed my letter to Andrew Smith, vice president of Innovation Partners, a management consulting firm. As part of my prework assignment for this workshop I had done extensive research on this company. My research included a meeting with John Dean, one of the firm's consultants. Small world—I was reintroduced to him by Margaret, the quality improvement manager with whom I'd information interviewed. While I was at Technology, Inc., John had helped us build collaborative work teams.

We agreed to meet at his office so that I could get a sense of the physical facility and the spirit of the work environment. I kept my eyes open, observing everything from the manner of the receptionist to the ways the consultants interacted with one another. John explained, "Because of increased global competition, our firm has been extremely busy meeting the needs of our corporate clients by focusing on innovation and productivity. The real challenge has been working on these issues while many of our clients were downsizing and restructuring." He proudly emphasized that they had an extraordinary client retention rate of 85 percent over the past twenty years.

Toward the end of our conversation, I said, "Tell me, what is your firm's operating philosophy?"

John responded, "Simply this: to grow with and serve the customer."

My challenge was to incorporate this information and other research into my marketing letter to Mr. Smith. Penny emphasized that writing a marketing letter was a *process* that involved writing, receiving feedback, and rewriting . . . and more rewriting. She suggested using a computer, which would be especially useful for rewriting.

During the next three days I focused on completing my marketing letter. After finishing the second draft, I put it aside for a couple of hours while I made some calls. After gaining some perspective, I looked it over again, one word, one sentence, one paragraph at a time. If a word didn't seem right, I consulted my thesaurus and dictionary. As I read each sentence, I would ask

Organizational Research: What Is Involved?

☐ The location or locations.

☐ The name of the founder, president, and other operating officers.

☐ The type of service/products the organization produces.

☐ The number of employees.

☐ Gross and net sales for the past three years.

☐ Who the competition is.

☐ How well this organization is doing compared to the competition.

☐ The name and title of the best person to contact regarding your needs. Some information about this person—for example, how long they have been there, what they do, some of their accomplishments, where they worked previously.

☐ The organization's business strategy.

☐ An awareness of the corporate culture.

☐ What some of the attributes are of successful people at your level.

☐ If and how the organization has distinguished itself in its market sector.

☐ What their newest product and/or service is.

☐ What is going on in the economy, country, state, community that may affect the organization.

☐ The organization's plans for the future.

☐ Meeting and talking with people who can give you information and insights about the organization.

☐ Reading everything that you can get your hands on about the organization, the market sector the organization is in, the outside forces influencing its business, and what makes people successful in the professional area in which you are interested.

myself, Am I really saying what I want to be saying about the company, about myself, and about what I can do for them? Is what I've *chosen* to say about myself the very best information I could have selected to pique the company's interest?

I followed Penny's advice: whether writing a resumé, a cover letter, or a marketing letter, don't send it without getting feedback. I faxed my letter to Mike Fielder for his review. First, I asked him for his general impression—for instance, "What do you think I'm trying to accomplish in my letter?" Then I asked for specifics—for example, "What would you change to make this better?" These questions helped give Mike some guidelines on which to focus his constructive comments.

Checking spelling, punctuation, and brevity, I made the necessary changes. Also, I perfected my proposal, clearly stating what value I would add to the firm and its customers. After the fourth rewrite, I sent it off.

Components of a Marketing Letter

1. State something you know about the organization.
   Example: I am impressed with your 85 percent client retention rate over the past twenty years.

2. Give them some information about you.
   Example: I have over _____ years of experience in the fields of management and management consulting. Specifically, some of my accomplishments include _____, _____, and _____.

3. Make a proposal that could boost their productivity.
   Example: I would like to propose a business relationship with your firm, tailoring TQM programs to the internal and external customer needs of computer manufacturers.

4. Take action.
   Example: I will contact you at the end of next week to follow up on your receipt of my letter and to determine if it would be beneficial for us to schedule a meeting.

August 9, 1992

Mr. Andrew Smith
Vice President, Quality Services
Innovation Partners, Inc.
100 Tradewinds Avenue
Boston, MA 02117

Dear Mr. Smith:

For the years that I have known of Innovation Partners, your firm has repeatedly and consistently been touted as a premier quality consulting firm. I have heard through some of your colleagues about the balance you strive for between conceptual frameworks and implementation focus. Having worked in a business whose customers relied on our service, I am impressed with your 85 percent client retention rate over the past twenty years. Clearly, these results are a testimony to your wisdom and your customer service.

I have over twenty years of experience in the fields of management and management consulting. Specifically, two of my accomplishments include the development of high-performing independent work teams and a worldwide network of managerial clients in our manufacturing divisions. My philosophy, as yours, is simply to grow with and serve the customer.

Given the increased demand for specialized quality consultants, I would like to propose working with Innovation Partners, full- or part-time, tailoring TQM programs to the internal and external customer needs of high-tech manufacturers. With my skills in leadership, management, and consulting as well as my allied values and extensive experience in the high-tech industry, I believe I could make a significant contribution to your consultant team and clients.

My intent is to develop a long-term relationship with you and your clients. I will contact you at the end of next week to follow up on your receipt of my letter and to determine if it would be beneficial for us to schedule a meeting.

Thank you for your consideration.

Sincerely,

Matthew Townden

Marketing Letter Writing Guide

Date: _____

Name: _____
Title: _____
Organization: _____
Address: _____
_____ Zip: _____

Dear _____:

1. State something you know about the organization.

_____

_____

2. Give some information about you.

_____

_____

3. Make a proposal that could boost their productivity.

_____

_____

4. Take action. *I will . . .*

_____

_____

Sincerely,

Although I tried to stop her, during the final week of interviews at the hospital, Lynda bought a bottle of champagne. As she proudly displayed the bottle, she said, "I can feel it. I know that you're going to get that job." I was afraid to admit it, but I thought so, too.

My last interview was with Dr. Stoute, the CEO, a man who embodied dynamic leadership. He believed that many of the old ways no longer worked, and he was looking for a "quality innovator" who had the inner strength to continuously reexamine values and try new methods. I assured him that many of my approaches in the past were creative and that I was looking for an organization in which habits could be challenged, making way for new approaches.

At the end of our interview he said, "Your candidacy looks good. If we decide to extend you an offer, Ms. Vilner will call you." Other than the two weeks when I had not heard from them, thus far there had been few surprises. Still, there had been no discussion regarding salary.

The most difficult part of this process was the waiting. I spent three full days (they felt like three full weeks), including the weekend, preoccupied with what the outcome would be. I thought, "That cork is ready to pop." Then Rita's voice would come to mind, "Not yet! Not yet!"

On Friday I checked with the secretary at Innovation Partners to find out when Mr. Smith would be in the office. She said he'd be in for a full day the following Monday. I changed my schedule to run at noon and go to the library at three. At 8:30 Monday morning, my call rang through to his direct line.

"Smith here, good morning."

"Good morning, Mr. Smith, this is Matt Townden." I paused for a moment. "Last week I sent you a letter that summarized my qualifications as a consultant and proposed how I could be of service to your firm."

"Mmmm, yes. What can I do for you?"

"I'll try to be brief. When I was a manager at Technology, Inc., I had the opportunity to work with one of your consultants, John Dean. Basically, he helped our work teams use their time more effectively, work more collaboratively, and become skilled problem solvers. As I stated in my letter, I am interested in doing similar work. With my background managing and consulting in high-tech, I feel that I could make a significant contribution to improving productivity in this sector."

Mr. Smith responded, "How much consulting have you done?"

"Quite a bit. I have a strong combination of internal consulting, and also during the past two years I've traveled internationally to consult with company divisions."

"Can you still travel? Our senior consultants are responsible for 50 to 60 percent billable time."

"Yes, I can. My wife works and my son is in college. During the past couple of years I traveled close to 60 percent. I enjoy traveling — I've taken my daily run in some interesting places!"

"I've got your letter on my desk. It sounds like you understand our philosophy. Why don't we meet next Monday morning? Let's say for coffee at 8:30."

"Thank you. I look forward to meeting you. I'll call on Friday to confirm with your secretary."

I hung up and yelled, "IT WORKED!" For a moment I looked out at the woods and thought, When I run, my feet will have wings. Before noon, I had time to send off a couple of thank-you notes and make a few networking calls.

When I returned from my run, the message indicator flashed two calls. One was from Ms. Vilner, who asked me to come in Tuesday morning at ten. The other was from Rita, who said, "It's time to negotiate salary!"

Rita had some similarities to John. One of them was her coaching ability. When I called her back, we both made an effort to keep our feet on the ground as we talked about salary negotiations.

"It's a myth that in a tough economy you'll *always* have to accept what is given you." She explained. "You've worked hard and can learn to negotiate so that you get what you deserve. Remember this golden rule: the person that mentions money first loses."

"Ah ha." I also thought, Rita likes to *win*!

Rita continued, "Win/win is when you get what you want and the other party is satisfied as well." Rita was reading my mind. We talked for the next twenty minutes about effective win/win salary negotiation strategies. I had done in-depth research on the organization, and Rita informed me about the current salary ranges for similar positions. I was clear that the job responsibilities were the challenges I was seeking and that the culture was a natural fit. I was told that the salary range was between $60,000 and

$70,000. During our conversation, I asked, "Rita, what if they offer me the lower end of the range?"

Rita replied, "Stay calm. Pause for a moment and say, 'I believe that you stated a salary range from $60,000 to $70,000. All other aspects of the job fit for both of us. I'd appreciate a salary closer to the top end of this range.'" Then she continued, "Matt, remain calm and say nothing. As tough as this will be, do not say anything. Wait for Ms. Vilner's gulp. When she breaks the silence, you'll get paid what you deserve."

I replied with a smile in my voice, "Rita, I'll wait for the gulp." Most important, I was clear that I was looking for a situation that rewarded me fairly—intrinsically and extrinsically.

On Tuesday morning, I reminded myself to stick with the issues and my interests. I was also keenly aware that I would need to see things from the hospital's point of view. They were experiencing financial constraints like most other employers but were committed to a long-term TQM strategy.

As Nancy Vilner approached, I greeted her with a smile. She shook my hand, but gave no smile in return. *I* gulped. Nancy shut the door and leaned forward in her seat, clasping her yellow pad.

"Matt, I tried to reach you this morning, but you'd already left. I'm sorry to give you this news, but an hour ago Dr. Stoute announced his decision to go with the internal candidate. He had a sleepless night, weighing the issues. What tipped the scale was the other candidate's knowledge of this culture and the relationships he had built with internal customers and our vendors."

"Boy, I can't believe it. I can't . . . I was so excited. We had a bottle of champagne waiting. Everything seemed so right."

"I'm very sorry. This decision had nothing to do with your skills or ability. You wouldn't have gotten this far without your outstanding qualifications. Competition among health care providers has increased the stakes. Dr. Stoute believed that the other candidate's ties within this organization and the health care community would expedite the implementation of programs."

"Oh. I'm disappointed."

"I can imagine. Finding a job, let alone one you really wanted, isn't easy."

"No it isn't. I've been at it for over five months." We were both silent for a couple of moments, then I said, "Who knows what will happen as the hospital changes. Would you keep me in mind for a position in the future?"

"Of course. I'd call you immediately."

Talk about a knock-out punch. It was hard to describe how I felt — lost, betrayed (again), and angry. How could I get so close and then *bang!* get shot down?

I didn't want to explain to anyone. As I walked through the park, I wondered if I'd ever find another situation that fit so well. It took so much effort to find this one. It went to show that no matter how successful the interviewing process seems to be, you never have the job until you receive the offer letter. Making it to third base was no guarantee that I'd make it home. This was a lesson I'd *never* forget.

When everyone else was working, midday seemed a strange time to be in the park. I felt lonely, but I wanted to be alone. My expectations had been as high as a kite. This job search certainly was full of reminders about keeping my feet on the ground and taking things step by step. A shadow fell over me, and I looked up from my bench. The man in front of me just stared at me. His hair was stringy and filthy, and his clothing was mismatched and worn. The look in his eyes said, I am lonely. As he cupped his hand, I simultaneously reached for some change. He took it and shuffled away.

My hunger pangs called me back from my thoughts. I checked the time — four o'clock. I must have been out of it for a while.

Lynda was beaming as I opened the door. "Things must have gone well, you're home so late."

"Honey, I have some awful news."

"Oh no."

"I didn't . . . I didn't get the job. At the last minute Dr. Stoute chose the internal candidate."

"Ohhh, but why? It was going so well. We thought you would get an offer today. I was so excited." Lynda put her head down and began to cry. "This is so unfair."

I put my arm around Lynda and said, "I know, I know."

We held each other until Lynda stopped crying, then I said, "The choice had nothing to do with my skills or ability. Dr. Stoute believed he needed someone who already knew the culture and had built customer relationships."

"It's still hard to believe. All indications were you had the job."

"I know. It will take a while to get over this one. At least Nancy Vilner was genuine when she said she'd call immediately about future positions."

"That's some consolation. Why were you home so late?"

"Oh, I needed to be alone and just felt bad for myself. I spent the afternoon in the park. An odd thing happened. I was feeling pretty down, and then a homeless man approached me at the park bench where I was sitting. In comparison, my circumstances didn't seem so bad."

"What do you mean?"

"Well, I'm certainly not down and out. Through my experience with the hospital, I've become more confident in my ability to interview. Also, I've got an initial interview lined up at Innovation Partners, and I have faith in my network."

Lynda sniffled and said, "And Matt, you've become extraordinarily resilient. I think I need a walk."

On the way out the door, Lynda turned and said, "Even though we're both tired of this job-search stuff, we'll manage. There's a great job out there for you."

I needed a couple of days to retrench, so I wrote in my journal, did some reading in preparation for my interview, and took a couple of long evening walks with Lynda. Without her, the downs of this transition would have been a lot more painful.

Key to my learning was that there were different paths to find meaningful work. I thought, I need to go back to the beginning and reexamine my values. What I most want is to have meaningful work, to contribute to and learn from others, to work with colleagues I respect and who respect me, and to earn a reasonable salary. I could certainly achieve these goals as a consultant. I didn't have to be a manager. Manager thinking was that old stuff about trying to stay on the career ladder—at any cost. In a smaller consulting firm like Innovation Partners, eventually I might contribute to the direction and the development of the business. It dawned on me that *pioneering* was my career theme. In every job at Technology, Inc., and in the companies before them, I was put in charge of new projects and often recognized the direction to head in next.

August 25

My Professional Goals

- *Do meaningful work — use my "pioneering" spirit and abilities to make a contribution to others and an organization.*

- *Join an organization that has a vision — one in which I believe.*

- *Contribute to and learn from a group of colleagues.*

- *Get fair financial compensation — between $50,000 and $70,000 depending on the situation.*

- *Work not more than fifty hours per week on average.*

- *Have between two and three weeks vacation per year.*

Regarding smaller business, I read in our local paper "Despite ongoing layoffs in many industries and a 7 to 9.5 percent national unemployment rate, new job growth is spurting at high-tech companies with fewer than 1,500 employees — especially manufacturers of biotech products, computer software, and environmental equipment." This information was in line with what I had learned in the SBM workshop. I had already been successful with the marketing letter approach and would use it again to increase my options as I researched and wrote to smaller businesses. It was two weekends before Labor Day, and on Monday I'd be meeting with Mr. Smith. Again, I wrote in my journal.

August 26

I felt sad about losing the TQM position at the hospital, but I can't afford to dwell on it. September being around the corner is usually a positive sign. After Labor Day the kids go back to school and companies seem to buckle down to business. I need to focus on my meeting with Mr. Smith.

My goal is to get a job in the TQM field. The hospital offered one way; Innovation Partners offers another. As George Bernard Shaw said, "The people who get on in this world are the people who get up and look for circumstances they want, and, if they can't find them, make them."

Depending on how our meeting went, I'd also let Mr. Smith know that I was open to a part-time position. Many consulting firms, especially in this economy, were hiring people part-time or on a project basis. This alternative kept down their overhead by reducing the costs associated with a full-time hire.

On Monday, I listened while Mr. Smith proudly talked about Innovation Partners. "Innovation Partners is a unique, employee-owned quality consulting firm. We believe in fostering our own learning as we foster our clients'. We've discovered over the years that it's not enough to hire the best talent. It's imperative that we also deliberately create learning forums for the development of our skills and to build a strong team."

"That sounds great in theory, but how is it practiced? All your consultants seem so busy."

"We are, but not too busy to share our collective know-how and who we are as individuals. On the last Friday of every month, we assemble into a company learning forum."

"No matter what is going on?"

"There are a few exceptions. Also, when consultants are in the home office or on assignment together, they frequently explore issues and talk about current methodologies. Learning is a significant part of this culture."

"Learning is what you sell to your customers."

"In a nutshell, yes, we do. We can't sell to our customers what we don't practice ourselves."

Mr. Smith deliberated for a moment and said, "I liked your marketing letter."

"Thank you. What did you like about it?"

"It was direct and to the point. You knew some things about us, and you let me know how your skills and background could benefit this organization. Most job seekers send a standard resumé and cover letter. That frustrates me. I'm too busy to figure out what they can do for us. That's like sending our marketing materials to a potential client, folding our hands, and hoping they'll call us. Rarely does that work."

I smiled, and Mr. Smith apologized for getting off on a tangent. He glanced at his watch, then handed me an "Associate Development Handbook."

"Matt, I'd like you to come back and interview with our team. This process involves twelve interviews, including two with

---

Taking Chances

Do's and Don'ts

DO . . .

- Tell your story—the one you've perfected—during interviews.
- Expand your options. Look into the "smaller business market" and various industry sectors.
- Thoroughly research organizations that interest you.
- Discover your career theme.
- Think about how you can benefit the organizations that interest you before you interview.
- Write your marketing letters to address the specific needs of the organization.
- Follow up on marketing letters you send.
- Keep on developing interviews, even when you're a finalist for a position.

DON'T . . .

- Expect others to bring out the best in you.
- Be unprepared for interviews.
- Confuse your job objective with your career theme.
- Think you have the job because you're going on a last interview.
- Give up.

---

support staff. Our aim is to discover if our core values match. Of course, skills and experience are essential, but values are at the heart of this organization. Our company was built on high ethical standards."

"I take it that this means that the group comes to a consensus decision on a candidate."

"Yes. The process will also require that you do a forty-five-minute presentation, after which there will be a two-hour period for you to ask us questions and for us to give you feedback."

"Sounds pretty thorough and challenging."

"It's a unique opportunity for all of us to learn and make an informed decision."

Mr. Smith exemplified the rigorous standards of Innovation Partners. His words, energy, and spirit were tremendously convincing. I was prepared to interview step by step. I was on first base, coming around to second! This situation, like the one at the hospital, would be another chance to learn and to demonstrate my ability. The answers would unfold through the process. I was committed to the lattice approach: developing other paths and investigating other opportunities.

10

Saying Thank You

You'll never be forgotten

Bingo! I got the job with Innovation Partners!

"A healthy cash flow," proclaimed Mr. Smith, "has contributed significantly to Innovation's longevity and enabled us, unlike other companies, to add staff." Given the precarious state of the economy, I accepted at an $8,000 pay cut. A compensatory clause in my employment agreement stipulated up to a 10 percent bonus based on organizational and individual performance. Rita may have thought I was compromising, but I had learned that the market called for flexible decision making. I made the decision to accept the job based on my personal priorities and an understanding of Innovation's needs. After all, I'd be doing work that I valued and, unlike so many others, Lynda and I would not have to relocate. I also thought, after I proved myself to the firm and the economy hopefully improved, I'd ask for more.

I felt fortunate and elated — and, I must admit, relieved. My new role as senior consultant would utilize my experience as a manager as well as my TQM skills. I'd no longer be a manager, I'd be a consultant helping individuals and organizations to change — as I had. You could say I'd gotten off the ladder and onto a lattice that works.

In our home hangs a painting by Diana Kan titled "Gentle Breeze." The painting portrays two shafts of bamboo bowing

---

Saying Thank You
Do and Don't

DO . . .

• Say thank you.

DON'T . . .

• Forget!

---

before a gentle breeze. One shaft is cut short, as though it had stopped growing, and the other shaft is long and vigorous, an image of boundless inspiration.

I like to think that the long bamboo shaft is a symbol of continuity, in contrast to the other, which appears to have died. For those who have lost their jobs, the process of securing another job is one that will include the "gentle breeze" of saying thank you. Even after you get your new job or open your new business, saying thank you will keep your network alive. Saying thank you is part of the energy of continuity.

It's good to keep a list of all those people who supported you by giving you ideas, leads, advice, and support. There are some you'll want to thank along the way. Everyone should be thanked after you land another job. People remember a thank you—and you cannot afford to be forgotten.

Saying thank you can be a lot of work when there have been many people supporting you, but it's important to do it. The payoff is great. Jackie found a job through the help of a friend. The friend had cut out an obscure ad from a town newspaper and sent it to her. This friend's thoughtful gesture was the connection that led to her current employment. Jackie sent her friend a note that simply said, "Thank you!" written a dozen times, down the length of a colored piece of paper. The note now hangs on her friend's office wall.

I sent Russ a simple note that said:

Russ,
I got a great job!
  Lynda and I are celebrating at the Ocean Grill in town. We would
be honored by the company of you and your wife. I'll give you a call.
                    Thanks for your support,
                    Matt

11

Going Beyond

Deepen your learning

Nine months ago I was struggling to survive. I had become one of those people who was certain that whatever happened, the company would always find a place for *me*. This learned expectation contributed greatly to my initial anger, frustration, and confusion on being laid off. I thought Technology, Inc., owed me a job. I had dedicated my expertise and years to managing people and projects, contributing to the profits of this organization. Never in my career had I been "kicked out." Always, *I* had left my employer for a better opportunity—more pay, increased responsibilities, a higher-level title.

In my new role as a consultant with Innovation Partners, I was assigned to a team. Our work involved helping two of our clients—one a computer manufacturer and the other an advertising agency—radically change the way work gets done, not just improve existing programs. This involved flattening the organizational hierarchies, a by-product of which was eliminating jobs. On the positive side, for the majority of remaining employees there would be greater autonomy, easier access to information across functional lines, and increased customer focus.

The part that churned my gut was eliminating jobs—firing good people. Believe me, it seemed necessary, made good business sense, and we were getting paid plenty for our TQM efforts.

The goal was to increase the quality of product and service and enhance sales. Part of the strategy involved downsizing, but sometimes I felt heartsick for the victims. At bottom, creating a new horizontal management structure and organizing the business around the customer meant laying people off. I had been there only nine months ago. The realization came crashing home to me: job loss was never easy — not for those losing their jobs, not for those remaining, not for those who did the planning for and implementing of a downsizing program.

I decided to visit John for a "tune-up" to talk about some of my feelings and to thank him personally for his guidance during my transition. As I entered the foyer of his office, I looked up the stairs that ended at the sunlit waiting area and I recalled my first session with John — his welcoming smile, my fear as I talked about losing my job, and my ambivalence as John introduced the lattice approach.

John greeted me with a warm handshake and said, "Great to see you . . . Congratulations."

I beamed and said, "Thank you. It's good to be here." As I sat in the chair facing the window, the worn leather arms felt familiar, and the sun warmed my face.

"How have things been going?"

"Oh, pretty well. I'm happy to have a new job, and for the most part, I'm feeling accepted by the other consultants."

John responded, "It takes time. You're the new guy. With everybody's busy schedule, especially in a consulting firm, I'm sure getting to know one another can become protracted."

"You have a point, although I have quickly felt at home, mostly due to work pressures demanding the cooperative efforts of our team."

"What kind of work have you been doing?"

"It's been interesting. That's part of the reason I'm here. The team and I have been working with two very different organizations — one a computer manufacturer and the other an advertising agency."

"They *are* different."

"Primarily, our work is to help these companies change their management structure from hierarchical to horizontal. Unfortunately, to do so, we're having to recommend and implement layoffs. Recommending these layoffs has been painful for me, and I want to figure out why."

There was a pause, then John asked, "Do you have any hunches?"

"I need to talk this out a bit. Some words come to mind like *scared, unfair, security,* and *learning.* These are just a few."

"Learning. What are some of the things that you've been learning?"

"Let's see . . . I've learned that I'm a good team player and that I can put my feelings aside to get the job done. I'm trusted by the senior execs, but I'm not so sure that I'm trusting them to the same extent."

"What do you mean?"

"Well, for the sake of running a business and doing it better, they'll lay off the most dedicated and loyal employee. If the person isn't or can't be useful within the flatter system, they'll let'm go. For example, at the agency we recommended streamlining customer service by putting the senior art director in direct contact with the customer. In so doing, this eliminated two account representative positions. We ended up dismissing one account rep who had been with the company for over nine years. They treated him okay — a six-month severance package, extended benefits — but still . . . "

"Matt, I think I'm getting the picture. Going back to your feelings, you've said that you've learned to put them aside in order to get the job done. I'm wondering if there's some way you can use your feelings more productively."

"How so?"

"Before I say much more, I'd like to ask you a question. What are you feeling insecure about?"

I felt a prompting inside myself, like the answer was struggling to come out even though I hated to admit it. I answered, "My job."

"Can you say more?"

"I think so. Basically, I'm identifying with the people caught in our downsizing efforts . . . no one's job seems secure these days. I thought that when I landed my job as a senior consultant, I'd have a reprieve. You know, like I was safe from all that job stuff for a while. I've been trying to believe it could be simple: do my job and I'd have a job." I took a tissue and wiped the sweat from my forehead.

"Matt, I agree, you're not only identifying with the people who are losing their jobs, but you're *over*identifying. I'd like to suggest that you strike a conscious balance between empathizing with their dilemma and doing your job. Try to look at it as though your client organization has hired you to help them change what is no longer working. Unfortunately, one requirement to make the necessary changes is to lay some people off. These people are fortunate that you're involved — you can empathize *and* you're in the position to advocate for the best termination process and packages possible."

"Mmmm. You have a point. I can influence their lives by making sure that they get treated in a better way than I was. John, you're right, I can have my feelings and feel for them. And I can also contribute in ways that will ensure more favorable transitions."

John paused, staring out the window. In a few moments he looked directly at me and said, "The rules have shifted; once you've lost a job and found another one, the journey hasn't ended. You may have reached a temporary home, but the responsibility will continue to be yours — to deepen your inner work and to strengthen and expand your external alliances. Of course, there's a greater chance that you'll retain your job if you're directly serving the customer or increasing sales, but today there are no guarantees."

Recalling Penny's workshop, I responded, "Basically, we are all self-employed."

"That's right; there's no free ride. Furthermore, I believe that you're talking about continuing to take responsibility for who you are, what you want, and for what and how you can contribute to others."

"You mentioned free ride — the computer manufacturer I referred to earlier is burdened by layers of unnecessary management. They're prime candidates for restructuring or a fatal fall."

"Matt, these managers will need to activate and expand their networks. Today that's simply part of staying employed and enhancing one's career."

"Networking . . . I'll need to continue networking."

"Yes, I agree. You'll need to network on three levels. First, talk with others about macro world issues — economic, political, and social — that are constantly affecting organizations and the individuals with whom you're working. Next, converse and read about your field, including up-to-date theories and strategies for implementing change. Finally, it will continue to be in your best interest to keep abreast of opportunities — in your current workplace and in the marketplace. And also, remember to listen. You'll learn a lot."

"Much of what you're saying I've heard before. Now that I'm in a different place, I needed to hear some of it again. I guess that's why I've been calling this meeting a 'tune-up.'"

John nodded. "Matt, this time we've agreed to meet for an hour and a half. During the last half of our session, let's go beyond your personal anxiety, deepen your understanding of how to become more effective at work, and examine some resources for building toward your future."

"So you mean going beyond a tune-up! What do you have in mind?"

"Well, I'll mention a couple of thoughts, and you can respond as you'd like."

"Okay."

"I've noticed that many who have lost a job and begin a new job work as though they were still afraid. *Fear,* much of it self-imposed, seems to be a primary motivator. This is true, I believe, of your experience."

"Mmmm. But, once you've been kicked out, that fear stays with you."

"Aha . . . For a moment, I'd like to continue with my thought. I'm not denying that losing a job and the difficulties of securing another in this competitive market can be very frightening experiences. Whether consciously or unconsciously, I believe too many people give fear a dominant position on their hierarchy of motivators. Fear becomes sort of a foundation for their thoughts and actions."

"John, you're talking as though people are *choosing* to hold onto their fear."

"Yes, that's exactly what I'm saying. I believe that some people aren't aware that they have a choice, that there are substitutes for fear."

"And if they had a substitute, they'd let go of their fear?"

"To different degrees, yes, though not completely. I think that some fear is healthy. On the other hand, fear doesn't have to be *the* reason for doing things."

"As you talk, I've been thinking what a strain and drain it is, and has been, to live with these fears."

"Which fears are you referring to?"

"When I lost my job, I was afraid our money would run out before I found another. I was also afraid of people's judgment and that I might fail. My fear mostly had to do with learning new things and with my expectations of myself. I expected to get things like networking, selling myself, and interviewing right the first time—you know, that Mr. Perfect stuff."

"Yes, I do know. What of your fears now?"

"Well, basically I'm afraid that with the economy and all, I might lose my job . . . again."

"Matt, I agree, it could happen, but why live with the fear that something might happen? Instead, I would *choose growth.* Since we've met, you have grown tremendously. I see you as vital—a word I use, and would like to use more often, for people who are *growing.*"

"So, let me understand. You're saying we can consciously replace fear with growth?"

"Yes, but I am also inferring that even with growth, we still can have, and often do have, fears. Fear is part of growth, but it doesn't have to be the reason for it."

"Mmm, I think I understand. Can you give me an example?"

"Yes, and I think one you'll appreciate. Do you recall the woman you saw coming out of my office, the one who was sad eyed?"

"I do. Quite well, in fact."

"Well, she is an artist—a very good one. She worked as an office manager with a small service firm. Although dedicated, she saw her job as a vehicle supporting her professional aspirations as an artist. When the firm filed for bankruptcy, she lost her job. Fortunately, she was given a small severance and within two months found work as professional secretary. Her new job offered her more money and better health benefits. She came in to see me because she had stopped using her evenings to paint. Instead, she was staying late at work."

"Maybe she had to."

"That's the point, she didn't. She was afraid of losing her job and compensated by staying late. She called it 'showing face'! After recognizing that she was operating predominantly out of fear, she began to look at how she could use her current situation as a springboard for her true joy—painting."

"How did things work out?"

"Well, she's much happier in her job. She's begun to sell her work commercially, and within the next couple of years, she plans to support herself as an artist."

"I imagine she still has some fears."

"Of course. But, she has reprioritized. Fear is simply a piece of the picture, not the major part. It's not the foundation on which her thoughts and actions are built. Matt, I'd like you to take this yellow pad and write down three words that capture what is most important to you professionally. Let's call them your 'core growth principles.' For example, creativity and autonomy are two that come to mind."

I thought, then wrote:

Pioneering, learning, integrity

"What have you written?"

"Pioneering, learning, and integrity. There are others, but these are the core."

"What does each mean to you?"

"Mmm . . . pioneering to me means the ability to create and establish new ground. Learning is continually finding ways to develop, stretch, and become better at my work. And integrity is simply being true to what I believe."

"I'm not surprised at your response, given what I know about you. My sense is that you, and others who recognize their core growth principles, notice that over the years they've remained the same, for the most part. What changes is your conscious awareness of these principles and your willingness, and often *need,* to act on what is most important to you. You've done this by deepening your understanding and turning your truth into action."

"You're talking about choice again. Also, I guess, I keep on evolving."

"Yes, if you allow it—if you don't let fear bury your growth." John went on. "If you'll recall when we first met, we talked about the traditional career ladder versus the career lattice approach."

"I remember."

"Right! You used many of the lattice approach principles for finding a job. Several of the same principles can also be applied for succeeding in the job you have—and hopefully for going beyond. When we began this session, you mentioned working with flatter organizations."

"Yes, as the world becomes more and more competitive, companies will become leaner and wider. They'll be learning to do more with fewer employees. Much of my job is to help them learn how."

"Okay, then what I'm going to share will be right on target. Bear in mind that since we first met, my intention has been to give you a greater awareness of choice and a framework for managing your career."

John handed me a copy of his "Prescription for Responsibility," explaining, "This prescription will help simplify what you'll need to do to enhance your career. It involves deepening your responsibility for your career choices and success, whether you have a job or you're looking for one. This brings to mind what Winston Churchill once said: 'The price for greatness is responsibility.' In turn the price for your security and career mobility is responsibility."

I briefly looked John's "prescription" over and responded, "You know, I've kept a notebook of all the different worksheets and handouts you've given me. I'm sure this will be a helpful addition. I've used a couple of them again since I've begun my new job. For instance, Life, Inc., has been a good reminder for reestablishing my support team. Thank you."

As we shook hands, John said, "Matt, remember, pace yourself. Growing and changing take time."

A Prescription for Responsibility

Going Beyond

BBI RESPOND

Believe—Believe in yourself.
You have special qualities and desirable skills for which a customer/company will pay you. Here are some ways you can deepen your belief in yourself:

1. Every time you complete a project give yourself a reward—take a walk, call a friend, or sit back for a moment to relax.
2. Accept a compliment without discounting it. Just say thank you.
3. Do the best job possible on the task at hand. Strive for excellence, not perfection, when networking, rewriting your objective, or researching a company.
4. Think of specific times when you've felt most alive and excited about your work. Ask, "Was I challenged?" "Why?" "What skills did I use?" "With whom did I work?" Now, look for opportunities in your current work or your job search where you can experience your aliveness again.
5. Accept projects and jobs that fit you and graciously turn down those that do not.

Basics—Go back to the basics.
The basics include:

- Identifying your three most important skills and writing several examples of each.
- Prioritizing your three most important values and explaining why.
- Clarifying what truly interests you—what gives you joy.
- The three Ps—practice, perseverance, and patience.

Innovate—Try different ways of doing things.
Never think in terms of one best way. For example, design a better resumé reflecting your current experience. Write a special interest article. Submit a draft to your boss, to some of your customers, and to a professional journal for their

A Prescription for Responsibility (*continued*)

review. Who knows; one of these ventures may land you another job or project or get your work published.

Risk—Try doing something new and different.
Plan and organize your steps, and then take action. For example, tell someone you don't know very well how you felt when you lost your job; accept a contract or an assignment even though you have little or no expertise; if you feel differently, disagree, even though others may be in agreement. In addition, continue networking. Now that you have a job, call and talk with someone you may have felt to be intimidating.

Energize—Focus on your strengths and add value.
Energize by reassessing your activities at the end of each day. Take fifteen minutes at the beginning of the day to think and plan. Contact people and companies that interest you. Remember Life, Inc.? Associate with people who support you. Also, learn from your colleagues; watch what they *do* that contributes to their success.

Smart—Work smarter, not harder.
You only have so many hours in the day for doing your job *and* preparing for your future. Here are some suggestions for working smarter:
- Establish goals.
- Ask questions. For example, ask people whom you respect for feedback about your work. Remember, ask how they think you could improve and what they think you do best.
- Continue to read about current developments in your field and areas of interest.
- Focus—break tasks down into manageable parts. For example, when writing a marketing letter, begin by stating something that you know about the organization and only *then* go on to the next part.

A Prescription for Responsibility (*continued*)

Promote—Sell yourself.
Selling yourself in the marketplace or in your workplace requires knowing yourself well and knowing specifically how
you can contribute to others (the Basics). In the workplace,
demonstrate your expertise by identifying needs and taking the
initiative to present a plan that could result in a solution.
Another way of selling yourself is to volunteer for projects
that others would rather avoid. Selling yourself more
directly involves telling your boss or a potential employer
what you're best at and how you could benefit them. Be sure
to back up your skills and benefits with relevant examples.

Open—Stay positive.
Keep and develop your sense of humor—a pressure valve
for releasing anxiety and other feelings. Things don't
necessarily happen when you most want them to. That's
life! Find the humor in your current situation, lighten up,
and progress toward your goal. Stay positive by assessing
before you judge. For example, after an informational interview, share your experience with friends or professional
colleagues; they may help you uncover an important piece
of information. Helping a friend or colleague is another
good way of developing a positive attitude. By listening to
someone else's issues, you can get some relief from your
own, help them, and feel better.

Nimble—Practice flexibility and add value.
If your goal is important to you and/or you've found a
place where you can add value, stick with it, but adapt as
is necessary to maintain it. For example, your goal may be
to work as the lead consultant for a major project. To
achieve this goal, first work with a top-grade team, then
ask to manage a smaller project. Experience your success
in scenarios that will incrementally lead you to your goal. If
you'd like to enter into a different type of work, volunteer
or work as an apprentice part-time. Don't give up your
goal; change how you get there.

A Prescription for Responsibility (*continued*)

Develop—Learning continues; it's your ultimate security. You can always learn a new skill or enhance one that you have. Successes and failures—as well as everything in between—are experiences from which to learn. To develop:
- Ask a question—"How can I do this better?"
- Come up with two or three answers to your question.
- Test your ideas in choosing your next step.
- Evaluate. Ask, "Does this possibility make the most sense?"

Go beyond. Whether you're earning a paycheck or not, the responsibility is yours for your future. Continue your active learning. Ask yourself and others "What does the company, department, and/or customer most need?" and/or "How do my skills and values best match with the work/marketplace?" Keep your eyes and ears open for the answer. Therein lies your opportunity—and theirs.

Over the next few days, I thought about John's prescription and realized that Eric, who had been working as a contract consultant while he sorted out his next move, was a likely candidate with whom I could start networking again. I gave him a call, and we agreed to meet for lunch at the Chinese restaurant in town. I looked forward to sharing stories and learning from his years in the business.

The waiter took our order for two wonton soups and chicken with cashew nuts.

As I poured the tea, I asked, "So you've decided not to join another firm?"

"You could say that that's part of the picture. As I've reassessed things, I've realized I've been feeling burned. When things went bad at my old company, they basically threw me out on my ear. I've decided to subcontract with three or four management consulting firms and spread the word that I'm available for work on a project basis."

"That way you'll most likely have more control."

"I hope so. I need to buy some time—to heal, to think things over. My work has afforded me mobility. I've worked with clients throughout the states. My wife and I have thought about moving. Who knows . . . contracting will give us time to sort things out."

"Sounds like a good plan, at least for now. How's the soup?"

"Hot! It's good."

"Eric, one of the reasons I wanted to meet with you was to discuss my own career growth. I know I've just begun a new job, but it's become clear that I need to continue to learn about my profession and about ways to enhance my career."

"I think I know what you mean."

"I'll be more specific. You've worked for three different management consulting firms, and I've just joined one. When you look back, is there anything you or your colleagues did to enhance your careers? And also, maybe a more difficult question, is there anything you wish you had done in your last job that might have prevented your layoff?"

These questions, I realized, were basically adaptations of the network questions that Jerry Brine had introduced to me. Here I was looking for similar information—behaviors and qualities that made people successful. There was one big difference—this time, I had a job!

"Actually, Matt, these are things I should be thinking about as well. I think I can answer both questions. First, I recall what some of the senior consultants would do to reduce their travel commitments. Many of them had built significant client bases during a five- to ten-year period. During this time they also had young families—you know, the old conflict between family and work."

"I've been there!"

"Well, these consultants had built significant financial clout in the firm. Two that come to mind had become increasingly frustrated with work/family conflicts. They didn't bother to negotiate for reduced travel schedules. Instead, they basically gave ultimatums."

"Ultimatums?"

"They said to the principals, 'Either you reduce our travel time or we're leaving.' They were so well entrenched with particular clients that there was little choice for the company but to comply."

"That type of strategy bothers me."

"Oh, me too. I brought up this example as one that worked under particular conditions. It's not one I'd personally feel comfortable with under any condition."

I thought for a moment about the importance I'd always placed on win/win outcomes. Ultimatums, especially for career enhancement, didn't fit for me.

"That's a good example of what can work for others, but it's one that neither of us would choose." I looked over at the cashew chicken and said, "Where did you learn to use chopsticks?"

"From T.V. . . . 'The French Chef!'" We both laughed.

"Let me tell you about some other strategies. Ones I know you'll appreciate. Although it may seem obvious, one is to do the very best job possible at the time. When working with a particular client, you're not thinking about the next client or the pile of work back at the office. Get my point?"

"I do. I've consistently found that by focusing on the business at hand, I not only deliver quality, but also, as a result, retain the client and often get referred to another."

"Yes, that's been my experience also. Here's another tip. I'd encourage you to have lunch or dinner on a regular basis with one of the principals, if possible, the president. I regret not having done that more myself."

"How regular?"

"I'd try to meet every two, maybe three months or so. It's one of the best ways to build rapport, show commitment, and learn about what's going on with the firm and its clients. Oh, I almost forgot, it's also an opportunity to let principals know about you and your work."

"Those are all good points. We get so busy consulting, it's easy to lose touch with the bigger picture as well as personal concerns."

"That's right. Looking back, that's one of the things that happened with me. I heard later that for some reason, the president didn't think I was committed to the business."

"How would he know? Most of the time you were off site with a client."

"That's the point. Busy is no excuse. It's my responsibility to keep the dialogue going as I change and as the organization changes."

"I like that word, *dialogue*. When I think back to Technology, Inc., I never really kept the dialogue going with Mr. Carroll and his cohort. I think I could have made more of an effort."

"How do you mean?"

"Let me see . . . I suppose my bosses got used to seeing me in one way and I got lazy. My dialogue—what I would say to them—rarely changed, even though I was changing and the organization was changing."

"What would you do differently?"

"I would have changed my dialogue. For example, I wanted management and leadership responsibilities to become a greater part of my job. I had had some experience, and I knew I had the potential. Mr. Carroll became accustomed to seeing me as the implementor—the guy who'd get things done. He wasn't around to observe my management and leadership efforts."

"So how would you change your dialogue?"

"Mmmm. Mr. Carroll was a nuts-and-bolts, statistics type of guy. So I'd talk in his language. I'd make a list of the *specific* examples that demonstrated my abilities as a manager and a leader. Of course, I'd also include the results."

"I see what you mean. You'd initiate conversations. Also, you'd change your dialogue, recognizing that he was a guy who made decisions based on facts."

"That's right. He wasn't one to trust anyone else's word. I would have given him the facts."

"I like that idea. It's another way to enhance your career. I've got another. Let me share it quickly, then I've got to leave. This builds on your idea about gathering facts and looking at evolving themes that are indicators of your career growth. I kept a business journal back at Management Strategies. It was not unlike your personal journal, but it focused on the documentation of key business events. Before I met with the president, I would review my journal for the contributions I had made and other details that could be useful in our discussions."

"Sounds good."

Business Journal

About your journal: Your journal is a way of documenting key business events. These events represent your success— the goals you've achieved, what you've learned, and how you've contributed to the company and your colleagues.

Every two or three months, look over your journal entries to determine how these events have or have not contributed to your career. Make note of what you've learned and some of the skills you've developed. Ask yourself how you can use this information to progress in your career and contribute to your organization.

Business Journal

Date: _____

Event (What was the specific thing that you did or accomplished?):

Experience gained (What encounters, training, adventures have you had?):

New learnings (What can you do now that you couldn't before?):

Assets/liabilities (Who/what was helpful? What were the obstacles?):

Results (What were the effects of your actions?):

Going Beyond
Do's and Don'ts

DO . . .

- Continue your learning—reexamine your feelings, network, and restate your goals.
- Recognize that you've begun a new transition.
- Think of yourself as "self-employed" and act that way.
- Continue developing a balanced life—work, family, recreation, financial planning, and so on.
- Keep a business journal.
- Meet with your boss on a regular basis.
- As necessary, change your dialogue.
- Try something new.
- Work because you want a challenge, because you want to grow and make a contribution.

DON'T . . .

- Think you've "landed" and that you're on safe ground.
- Ignore your responsibility to yourself.
- Think or act as though your employer will take care of you.
- Work out of fear.

"Sorry, Matt, I've got to run. I'll send you a business journal outline."

My fortune cookie read, "Now is the time to try something new."

That evening I wrote in my journal.

November 24

The goal is not reached when I get a job. Transition has not ended: I still feel some confusion, new goals emerge, and reexamination and networking continue.

After meeting with John and Eric, I felt relief, but mostly renewed courage and commitment to continuing my journey. When I lost my job, there were no benefits, at least none that I could see. Today, on the other hand, and for the rest of my life, I've learned that I'm responsible for my destiny. I may not always be in control of my destiny, but I have the power of choice. As long as I'm willing to take responsibility, I can ask a question, find an answer, and take action.

Resources

*Information for managing job loss,
finding work, and going beyond*

Contents

Introduction

The intent of this resource section is not to overwhelm but to inform and to suggest tools for dealing with job loss and enhancing your career mobility. Losing your job is confusing and mystifying enough without adding an overwhelming choice of resources and references.

I have chosen materials that, over time, I've successfully shared and used with others in career transition. These materials offer means to support and reawaken your head *and* your heart during a crucial time in your life—a time of letting go, dealing with intense feelings, and sorting out conflicting issues and interests. These resources and references will also help you rethink old strategies and map out new ones—strategies that will make sense and work in a changed world. For many, today's world is quite different from the one you negotiated years ago during your last career transition/job search.

Most city and town libraries are an outstanding source of information and support. As part of your transition, plan to visit your local library three times a week. Doing so will provide structure to your day, and you will encounter helpful librarians who can lead you to directories, publications, and associations that can give you direction and save you time and money.

Today, people who have lost their jobs should not be viewed as a distinct group, but rather as part of the employed. As the saying goes, "I have a job; it is finding a job." For many, the primary difference is a paycheck. All workers must be prepared, whether they're earning a paycheck or not, to go beyond their current situation. Whatever you're doing now won't last; the world is changing quickly for all of us. To cope with these changes, information in this section ranges from answers about severance and who to go to for help, to the ins and outs of unemployment insurance. For your head and your heart, some of the readings suggested include *Your Rights in the Workplace,* by Dan Lacey; *Tran-*

sitions, by William Bridges; *Parting Company,* by William Morin and James Cabrera; *Mindfulness,* by Ellen Langer; *Jobs 92,* by Kathryn and Ross Petras; *Good Works,* by Jessica Cowan; *The Age of Unreason,* by Charles Handy; *The Fifth Discipline,* by Peter Senge; and, of course, *What Color Is Your Parachute?* by Richard Bolles.

These are resources for deepening your learning and going beyond your current situation, whether you have a paycheck or not.

ACKNOWLEDGMENTS

The information in this resource chapter was made available through the advice, counsel, and generosity of many busy professionals. I'd like to thank everybody who contributed, especially, John Marre, assistant director of labor relations, Department of Employment and Training, Boston; Maida Shifman, director of customer service, Department of Employment and Training, Boston; Ellen Messing, partner/lawyer, Shilepsky, Messing & Rudavsky, Boston; Leslie Borden, senior consultant, Right Associates, Boston; Les Combs, consultant for client services, Right Associates, Boston; Meryl Bralower, work/life consultant, Newton, MA; Anne Schnoebelen, assistant director, National Employment Lawyers Association, San Francisco, CA.

Section A
Terms and Tools

This section defines working terms and practical tools for dealing with the issues related to job loss, career transition, and job search. The terms and acronyms in the glossary have been redefined and created to be useful to you. The definitions are not taken from Webster's, but instead are constructed from the experiences of people who have been successful negotiating job loss through to finding other jobs.

Glossary

Attitude.   The way you think and what you believe. For example, "I feel inspired; what I don't know, I can learn."

Base hits.   Smaller successes that lead to your larger goal. Refer to page 64.

BBI RESPOND.   A prescription for taking responsibility leading to achieving your goals in the workplace and the marketplace. (Described in detail on pages 165–68.)

Career ladder.   A traditional system for career advancement based on moving "up"; usually found in mid–size or larger organizations.

Career lattice.   A nontraditional system for career "enhancement" based on mobility in a variety of directions. Using this system, the job seeker can step in any direction, going to either side or up or down within the workplace or the marketplace. *See also* Lattice approach.

Career theme.   Represented by words, phrases, and feelings that have repeated throughout your career. For example, "helping others," "developing new ideas," or "making better what someone else has started." Think of it as a melody you've played — in the jobs you've had, in the projects you've completed, and in the roles you've assumed, both professionally and personally. (Refer to pages 138–39.)

Chronological format.   An accounting of your employment history, beginning with your most recent position. This resumé format usually includes your objective; your experience, with a brief description of your responsibilities; dates of employment; education; and professional affiliations. (Refer to pages 103, 106.)

Competency.   A skill, such as problem solving or networking, that increases your ability, in this case, to conduct a successful job search. (Refer to page 43.)

Control.   Mastery of one's thoughts and actions for the purpose of bettering one's life and contributing to the lives of others.

Customer focus.   Listening and responding to the needs and the wants of the customer. If you're looking for a job, your customer is the organization and their customers. If you're starting a business, you'll need to determine who your customers are and analyze their needs. In either case, thorough research is required — doing homework on a company's culture, why people buy the company's product, why a customer would be interested in buying your product/service.

Facilitator.   An individual who uses his or her skills with individuals or groups to guide them to discover insights and opportunities for personal, professional, and/or spiritual growth.

Feedback.   Information derived from your experiences and the world at large as well as evaluation of your performance passed on to you by others. Using this information can result in change and growth.

Flexibility. The ability to revise plans, create options, and adapt to circumstances. If you've found a meaningful goal, stick with it. If you are in the process and encounter difficulties, change your approach, revise plans, and create other options.

Focus. To establish a direction, even if it is as small as knowing what step to take next.

Functional format. Action/results statements organized under your resumé's primary skill headings. Each statement should speak to one of your capabilities and accomplishments. The purpose of the functional format is to give you the freedom to select specific examples of your experience and to arrange them in such a way that supports your objective and the needs of your customer (the organizations you have targeted as prospective employers). (Refer to pages 103, 107.)

Goal. Something you are aiming to do; an aspiration.

Inner work. Those areas of development, such as skills, personality, values, and attitude, that require more internal examination as you negotiate your job/career transition.

Inverted doughnut. A term coined by Charles Handy, author of *The Age of Unreason.* He uses this analogy to help you analyze to what degree you would want part of your work to be a defined job description and to what degree initiative, creativity, and opportunity are important in your work. For example, the majority of a bank teller's job involves a tightly defined job description that allows little room for making changes in scheduling or in how the work gets done. On the other hand, an "inverted doughnut" depicting the job of a professional salesperson would show the opposite picture: substantial opportunity to initiate change and innovate depending on customer needs, with a less defined job description. (Refer to pages 181–82.)

Journal writing. A private way of expressing and clarifying your thoughts, observations, feelings, and goals. In addition, journal writing can give you a sense of purpose when you're going through a job loss/career transition. (For personal journal, refer to pages 42, 45, 55, 131, 133. For business journal, refer to pages 171–72.)

Lattice approach. The idea that career mobility is built on the notion of a *lattice,* not a ladder, thus affording the career/job changer greater freedom. When using this system, self-management, a commitment to learning, and creativity are encouraged. Thus, in a changed and continually changing workplace and marketplace, you will be able to increase your number of career options and expand the ways in which you can achieve your goals. (Refer to pages 3–4, 35–37, 43, 189, 190.)

Layoff. Being relieved of one's job; a difficult circumstance that can unfold into an opportunity to engage in self-discovery, renewal, and a promising work life.

Leaderless support group. A group of three to six people whose goal is to emotionally support, encourage, and mobilize one another toward each individual's goals. Rather than having a leader run the group, it is managed by agreed-on guidelines. The purpose of these guidelines is to give members just enough structure for clarifying goals, expanding options, and taking risks. (Refer to pages 90–92.)

Learning. To continue vitally growing and changing throughout your life.

Life, Inc. The idea that we are all running a company called Life, Inc. (your life), in which you are head of the board of directors. It's your primary job to run Life, Inc., in the black (profitably). Part of your obligation is to select board members who support, challenge, and guide you toward your goals. (Refer to pages 38–39.)

Listening. Actively hearing what others have to say.

Meaningful work.   Work that feels natural and is rewarding. This work would be fulfilling and challenging and pay you fairly for your productivity and contributions. In this work, you should be able to use your true qualities and skills and to further develop them.

Natural fit.   Meaningful work—work that is in harmony with who you are and what the marketplace needs at a particular point in time.

Networking.   The active development and careful use of contacts for professional and personal enhancement.

Networking referral sheet.   A document sent to associates and colleagues, accompanied by a self-addressed stamped envelope, for the purpose of encouraging contact referrals and job leads. (Refer to pages 99–100.)

Outer work.   Those concerns, such as finances, networking, and interviewing, that are more external to the search process.

PAL.   A technique used to increase your networking ability. PAL stands for:
    P = Purpose: The aim of your call or meeting.
    A = Agenda: One or two topics you'd like to discuss.
    L = Limit: The amount of time you intend to spend talking or meeting.
PAL is a tool that maximizes your probability for success by keeping you focused and organized. It is a method that will let your contact know that you won't waste his or her time or complicate information gathering with asking for a job. (Refer to pages 74–78.)

Patience.   Keeping calm and enduring throughout a difficult time.

Perseverance.   Sticking with a process until a task or project is completed.

Prescription for responsibility.   *See* BBI RESPOND.

Prioritize.   To decide what is important. To become successful, everything cannot be of equal importance; prioritizing will help you focus on the most important. For example, your priority may be to find meaningful work and to spend time with your family. To meet this goal, a priority would be to find a job with limited overnight travel. Most likely, this would rule out the majority of external senior consulting positions.

Recruiter/search consultant.   A professional who matches the employment needs of the corporate client with talent in the marketplace. (Refer to pages 114–15, 119–21.)

Research.   Gathering, analyzing, and synthesizing information about who you are, what you want, and about the marketplace and specific organizations. The purpose is to deepen your personal understanding and to clarify your needs. In addition, research will lead you to expand your network and to gain invaluable facts and insights about the marketplace and organizations that interest you.

Responsibility.   The ability to take charge in one's life by solving problems, making choices, taking action, and committing to one's goals.

Reward.   Payment for partially or fully completing a task or project. Payment can be in a variety of forms, including money, a product, and/or an experience.

Risk.   Making a trade-off of what you know for a potentially better situation. Taking a risk involves planning, researching, prioritizing, evaluating, and ultimately taking action. For example, before you drove a car, you prepared for this risk by learning, planning, and practicing.

SBM.   *See* Smaller business market.

Security.   Self-knowledge, the ability to learn, the resourcefulness to create and materialize one's goals.

Self-employed. Creating, directing, and managing one's own liveli-hood in such a way that you and your customers are satisfied.

Self-esteem. Valuing yourself or having self-worth. Feeling healthy, creative, loving, and productive.

Self-management. Taking full responsibility for your career, in-cluding clarifying and prioritizing your skills and values and thoroughly researching the needs of organizations or the type of business that interests you. (Refer to pages 63–64, 65–66.)

Severance. Payment to an employee on termination of her or his job or contract. Severance payment is not an entitlement; it is intended as an income bridge from your past job to your next job. A severance package can include options that range from extended health benefits to a regular paycheck for an agreed-on period to outplacement counseling.

Skills. Abilities that enable you to perform in a credible manner.

Smaller business market (SBM). Organizations employing fewer than 2,500 employees. Since 1987 the greatest job growth has been in the SBM sector. (Refer to pages 136–37, 150.)

Story telling. Talking with people who will *listen,* not offer judg-ments, about your loss, fears, and abilities. By telling your story, you'll have the opportunity to share your feelings, then name them. Second, you can filter out what you do and don't want to share with a potential employer. (Refer to pages 34–35, 36 (box), 38–41.)

Success. Achieving a favorable outcome and feeling challenged about the process of getting there.

Support. Sustenance, companionship, and professional aid that help one feel better and stronger. Support that works gives you the courage and strength to clarify who you are, what you want, and ways to achieve your goals.

TAP. A method for achieving goals and rewarding yourself along the way. TAP stands for:

> T = Task: A specific job you need to do.
> A = Action: What you'll do to get what you want.
> P = Payoff: The way(s) you'll reward yourself for tak-
> ing action.

With job loss and career transition can come an overwhelming number of converging needs that often result in your feeling stuck and afraid. TAP helps you mobilize and enables you to focus on one task, to take action, and to reward yourself for your efforts. (Refer to pages 111, 112.)

Total quality management (TQM). This method, currently being adopted by many companies, targets satisfying customers' requirements and expectations as well as the individual needs of employees. (Refer to page 92.)

TQM. See Total quality management (TQM).

Transition. The journey between two worlds: the one you left and the one to which you're going. For many, this is a time of chaos and fear of the unknown. But it can also be a time of creativity, learning, realignment of values, renewal of energy, and new experiences.

Trimtab. A miniflipper attached vertically to the stern of the rudder of a boat. When the trimtab is maneuvered even slightly, it will change the course of the boat. Thus, making small changes can shift your direction. (Refer to pages 108, 109.)

Trust. Faith in oneself and in others. A belief that things will work out in your life.

Volunteering. An opportunity to explore other job/career possibilities. For example, in your past job you may have been a business administrator. Now you may want to explore jobs in health care. If so, volunteer in a local health facility. Volunteers get offered jobs!

Career Lattice Approach

- Take responsibility.
  Commit to discovering and managing your own path.

- Focus on the situation or task at hand.
  Break a task down into doable parts. For example, refer to PAL for networking.

- Do your inner work.
  For example, tell your story—sort out, express, and name your feelings.

- Do your outer work.
  Sell yourself—add value to the customer/company.

- Expand your options.
  For example, practice flexibility. Keep your goal, but explore different paths as a means to achieve it. Remember, climbing the traditional career ladder is only one option.

- Never stop learning.
  Deepen your inner work, ask questions, and expand your external alliances.

How to Use the Career Lattice Approach

Career Lattice Approach	How It Works	Example	How It Might Work for You
1. Take responsibility.	Ask for support to build your inner strength and explore external options.	Use "Life, Inc.," as a means to identify who and what might be supportive to you. Begin by telling your story to a friend who will listen.	
2. Focus on the situation or task at hand.	Commit to the step-by-step process of solving problems and completing tasks. Follow through on what you begin.	Break down the writing of your resumé into doable parts. For example, a. Objective b. Experience c. Education d. Professional affiliations e. Capabilities and accomplishments	
3. Do your inner work.	Engage in ongoing self-discovery. Identify, clarify, and give examples of your skills, values, and interests.	If you have identified sales as one of your primary skills, then list examples that support your ability in this area. Begin each example with a verb that expresses your ability.	
4. Do your outer work.	Reserch companies that interest you.	Send for the company's annual report and look through library periodicals for additional information.	
5. Expand your options.	Practice flexibility. Remember, climbing the traditional career ladder is only one option.	You may have been a manager of training within a larger company. If you want to continue in the training field, consider consulting externally or internally, working part-time as a consultant and the rest of the time as a professor, or looking for a management position but in a different part of the country.	
6. Never stop learning.	Give yourself permission to learn, discovering new ideas and testing those ideas. Learning is an ongoing process. Learning works best when you ask yourself, "How can I improve?" "What is my next best step?" "Who can I contact to check out my ideas?" Do this several times a day.	When you're interviewing, don't prejudge whether you fit or not. Give yourself time to make a determination based on your learning.	

Section B

Nuts and Bolts

This section tells you what to do if you have questions about:

- Dispelling discriminatory myths
- Legal issues
- Severance agreements
- The ins and outs of unemployment benefits
- Who to go to for help

In the event that you've lost or might lose your job, this section is intended to give you answers to some important questions. It will also direct you toward professional help appropriate to the stage of job loss you're experiencing. These professionals can help you protect your rights, believe in yourself, discover your skills, and uncover jobs. Most importantly, this section is designed to give you information and tools that will help you make educated choices, overcome hardships, and mobilize your career.

Dispelling Discriminatory Myths

First, I have included this information in order to validate what many older workers already know but may be apprehensive to articulate: *they are flexible, loyal, and productive beyond most employers' perceptions.* Second, this section is intended to heighten the awareness of employers who have any doubts about the virtues of hiring older workers.*

*Released in May 1991, this information was provided by John Gormley, director of business partnerships with Operation A.B.L.E. of Greater Boston and the Commonwealth Fund. The Commonwealth Fund is a national organization, founded in 1918 by Anna M. Harkness, dedicated to improving the common good by studying the health and well-being of Americans.

1. *Myth:* Older workers are less productive, efficient, and motivated than younger workers.
   Fact: Research shows that in most jobs, productivity remains constant until well after retirement age.
2. *Myth:* Older workers are inflexible and resistant to change.
   Fact: Research shows that such behavior is not age related and that older workers want to keep their skills and knowledge current.
3. *Myth:* Older workers cannot be trained in new technologies.
   Fact: In one study, older workers were trained to operate sophisticated computer software in the same time (two weeks) as were younger workers.
4. *Myth:* Older workers cost more to employ and cannot work as efficiently as younger people.
   Fact: Older workers stay on the job longer than do younger ones: three years versus one year, with resulting savings in average training and recruiting costs per hire of $618 versus $1742 for younger workers.
5. *Myth:* Older workers are inflexible about the terms of their employment, such as working full-time or overtime.
   Fact: Research shows that older workers participate in all three shifts and overtime.

Legal Issues

You can lose your job for many reasons—laid off, fired, early retired, relocated, demoted, unchallenged, disabled—and each cause raises various legal issues. Job loss or change, regardless of the circumstances, is often painful. The pain that can be hardest to bear, according to Ellen Messing, a partner in a Boston law firm, "is if you believe you've been singled out because of personal characteristics, such as your age, that have absolutely no correlation with your value as an employee."

Generally, there are two primary reasons to meet with a lawyer:

1. To determine if termination gives rise to legal claims. Were you treated fairly, given the circumstances?

2. To determine if what you've been paid is fair. Should you sign the severance offered you?

Many workers also meet with a lawyer *before* they might lose their jobs. In this case, the worker may have heard of a coming layoff or that older workers are being replaced by a younger work force.

When seeking legal assistance, choose a "plaintiff employment lawyer," one who exclusively represents the employee, not management. Hopefully, you will receive sound advice concerning the next steps to take. The National Employment Lawyers Association in San Francisco, founded in 1985, is a national association of 1,300 plaintiff employment lawyers. These lawyers handle cases involving wrongful termination, employee discrimination, employee benefits, and others. Send a self-addressed stamped envelope for more information to National Employment Lawyers Association, 535 Pacific Avenue, San Francisco, CA 94133. Be aware that this association does not give legal advice on the phone.

Your Rights

You do have rights, including:

1. If an employer fires you without just cause, you may have grounds to sue. You should seek legal advice.

2. If you are fired, laid off, or unchallenged (choose to leave your employer for a better opportunity), the law gives you the right to use the skills and experience you have gained.

3. "Agreements not to compete," according to Melvin Belli, attorney at law, "are enforced only if the restrictions are reasonable in terms of time, activity, and geographical area. An agreement that bars you from engaging in any type of business in any given part of the United States for the rest of your life is invalid; you've got to be able to make a living."

4. If you are fired you *may be eligible for certain benefits,* such as severance pay.

5. If you are laid off, the amount of benefits you receive de-

pends on the company policy or union contract, unless otherwise stated in the company policy.

6. If you are fired, you may have legal right to notice. Check into the company's policies.

Eleven Action Steps

Take (or avoid) the following steps as soon as you learn of your termination:*

1. *Don't sign anything without legal advice.* Your employer may offer you salary continuation, severance pay, or continuation of benefits in exchange for signing papers in which you agree to give up your legal rights. Fight the temptation to sign whatever it takes to "get it over with." You may be able to obtain a significantly better bargain after obtaining legal advice.

2. *If at all possible, see a lawyer right away.* Very short deadlines apply to most claims for age discrimination, so you should see a lawyer as soon as possible after you learn of your discharge. If you have any thoughts of suing, you need to make sure what you say and do is consistent with your legal strategy. Even if you do not think you want to sue, a lawyer can help you formulate a strategy for leveraging the best possible settlement with your employer.

3. *Formulate your goals.* Are you prepared to hold out for a large monetary award, which may take years of litigation? Or is it more important to obtain a settlement right away? Are there nonfinancial benefits you seek, such as clearing your personnel file?

4. *Assemble your records.* In order to pursue your claims, you will need to put together a set of critical records and papers reflecting the history of your employment. Some of the more important records to gather include:
- all your past performance evaluations
- your job descriptions

*These steps were contributed by Ellen Messing, a partner in the Boston law firm of Shilepsky, Messing & Rudavsky, which concentrates in the representation of employees and labor in all aspects of the employer-employee relationship.

- your termination paperwork
- your company's personnel manual or employee handbook
- your collective bargaining agreement, if you were a union member
- copies of your applications for new jobs

5. *Talk with other termination victims.* Other employees who were discharged or pressured into resigning may have useful information to offer. Some may even be interested in jointly pursuing legal action with you, especially when a number of employees were injured by one corporate action (such as layoff or reduction in force).

6. *Seek unemployment compensation.* Most discharged employees are entitled to collect unemployment benefits under state law. You should apply for benefits at your Employment Security Agency promptly, since your allotment-of-benefit weeks start as soon as you are discharged, not at the time you first seek benefits. Don't be embarrassed to apply; this is a benefit you've earned.

7. *File claims with governmental antidiscrimination agencies.* Whether or not you have a lawyer, you can and should file a discrimination complaint with the federal and state agencies in charge of administering the antidiscrimination laws. The federal Equal Employment Opportunity Commission (EEOC) investigates and attempts to conciliate claims of age, race, sex, religion, and national origin discrimination in employment.

8. *File complaints, if warranted, with other governmental agencies.* Many federal and state agencies have antidiscrimination or other mechanisms in place to secure the rights of discharged workers. For example, in Massachusetts, the Department of Labor and Industries enforces the following laws:

- a nonpayment-of-wages law (which requires employers to pay employees all accrued salary and vacation pay on termination)
- a personnel records law (which requires employers to provide employees with copies of their personnel files and to permit employees to correct errors in the files)
- aspects of a new corporate takeover law (which requires many employers to pay employees two weeks' pay per year of service if they are terminated as a result of an actual or attempted corporate takeover)

9. *Send a demand letter.* You can do this either through a law-yer or on your own. Often, employers who are advised that a strong claim could be brought against them are willing to settle out of court. This is more likely to occur if a lawyer sends a let-ter, but even your own carefully drafted letter may cause the com-pany to consider settlement.

10. *Seek support services.* If you pursue legal action, or even if you don't, this job loss period is likely to be very stressful for you. You may need the support of a clergy member, physician, psychologist, or marriage counselor. To seek such services does not indicate weakness. Instead, it often helps encourage the in-sight you need to achieve your goals.

11. *Look for a new job.* If you sue, you may need to demon-strate that you pursued a new position in order to prove that your ex-employer, and not any lack of effort on your part, is respon-sible for your economic losses. You need not accept a job that is unreasonably inferior to your old job.

Sources of Legal Information and Advice

BOOKS

Every-Body's Guide to the Law, by Melvin Belli and
Allen P. Wilkinson (New York: Harper & Row, 1987).

Written in common language, this is an excellent resource for more information on noncompete agreements and other em-ployee-/work-related issues such as who owns inventions or copyrights developed at work or the misuse of an employer's con-fidential information. Refer to chapter 11, "Employees."

You and the Law: A Consumer Guide Book, by the American
Bar Association (New York: Signet Reference, 1991).

Also written in lay terminology, this guide uses a question-and-answer format to provide answers to your "out-of-work" questions. Following is a sample from this book:

Q. What is the difference between laying off and firing a worker?
A. This can be very important. Firing a worker ends the employer/employee relationship, usually because the employer judges the employee to be inadequate. The employee may be eligible for certain benefits. One such benefit is severance pay. However, the worker may lose eligibility for others, such as insurance.

When laid off an employee can be considered satisfactory, but the layoff may occur because of a work shortage or economic problem. A layoff may be temporary. It also may be for an indefinite period. If it is quite long, it can effectively end the working relationship. The amount of benefits received depends upon company policy or the union contract. Layoffs imply that the employees will be back at work if the company expands the workforce again. However, layoff policies contain a cutoff point. After that point, a worker loses any seniority or re-employment rights.

If told by an employer not to come in, employees should find out whether the employer has laid them off or fired them. They also should ask about their legal rights.

ORGANIZATIONS

American Bar Association (ABA)
750 North Lakeshore Drive
Chicago, IL 60611
312–988–5555

Call for a booklet using local lawyer referral services by state and county. Many state bar associations will also give legal referrals.

American Arbitration Association
140 West 51st Street
New York, NY 10020 (headquarters)
212–484–4000

The American Arbitration Association, founded in 1926, is a public-service, not-for-profit organization with approximately thirty-five offices across the country that is dedicated to resolution of disputes of all kinds through the use of arbitration, mediation, democratic election, and other voluntary methods. Among disputes covered are automobile accident, commercial, community, labor, and international claims. Send for their guide to mediation and arbitration.

Tele-Lawyer
19671 Beach Boulevard, Suite 207
Huntington Beach, CA 92648
800–835–3529

This private law firm offers legal advice over the phone at a $3.00-per-minute charge. Staff will also review documents, such as employment contracts. Hours are from 8 A.M. to 6 P.M. PST.

Severance Agreements

A severance payment is a payment to an employee on termination of her or his job or contract. Severance payment is not an entitlement; it is intended as an income bridge from your past job to your next job. A severance package can include options that range from extended health benefits, to a regular paycheck for an agreed-on period, to outplacement counseling.

According to the American Bar Association in *You and the Law* (1991):

> An employer must give severance pay if there are contracts or collective bargaining agreements that provide severance benefits. Employees at-will usually must rely on their employer's generosity. However, some state laws require severance pay under certain conditions.
>
> An employee at-will may lose their job without notice and for any reason or no reason at all. An employee at-will usually works in the private sector.

Severance Guidelines

There is no standard severance package, although some guidelines do exist. Generally, if there are no preexisting conditions—

contracts, collective bargaining agreements — there are four primary factors that will determine your severance.

1. Length of service — how long you have been with the organization.
2. Compensation — how much you were earning.
3. Level — your position with the organization.
4. Goodwill — how generous your ex-employer decides to be.

Some state laws require severance under certain conditions, but most workers must rely on their ex-employer's generosity. Remember, whatever you are offered, you always have the choice to negotiate for a different package. Some severance options are listed on page 200.

If you negotiate a "lump sum" severance, then you can, after five working days, apply for unemployment insurance. As long as you are receiving weekly severance pay from your ex-employer, you may not be eligible for unemployment insurance. Check with your state's employment security agency or with a lawyer.

Sometimes, you stand a better chance of negotiating a lump sum payment if your former employer is a smaller firm. This is because the employer may be financially incapable of paying out multiple severances over several months. To enhance a smaller package and to promote goodwill, your ex-employer may agree to a lump sum payment.

If you do receive a lump sum payment, it will be your responsibility to manage this sum. When you receive payment, develop a financial plan. Talking with your spouse and consulting a financial adviser can give you ideas about how to manage and stretch your dollars.

Severance Options

If your employer does not have a formal severance policy, you may want to consider the following as options for negotiations:

☐ Lump sum severance
☐ Regular paychecks for an agreed-on period
☐ A closed-ended severance agreement, with an option to extend
☐ An open-ended severance agreement
☐ Extended health benefits
☐ Outplacement counsel
☐ Financial assistance for technical retraining
☐ Financial assistance for college courses
☐ Financial assistance for moving household goods
☐ Use of a computer and printer
☐ Office space
☐ Use of phone and message services
☐ Access to secretarial staff
☐ Professional references
☐ Programs you've developed that you'd like to take with you
☐ Nullification of a noncompete contract
☐ Use of the company's on-line data base
   Other:
☐ _____
☐ _____
☐ _____

The Ins and Outs of Unemployment Benefits

Provided by all states, "unemployment benefits" refer to two services: (1) unemployment insurance, and (2) employment services
(job/career counsel, job placement, and so on). Both federal and
state governments have important responsibilities for unemployment benefits. A major federal responsibility is to finance all federal
and state administrative costs of unemployment benefits and to
ensure that funds granted to the state for administration are ex-
pended properly and efficiently. The program is administered pur-
suant to state law. State agencies differ greatly and are listed under various names, although all offer these two distinct services:
unemployment insurance and employment services.

Unemployment Insurance

WHAT IS IT?

Unemployment insurance (UI) is income. The aim of this service is to provide workers and their families income when they are out of work through no fault of their own.

Every state has a maximum weekly amount that an out-of-work person can collect. In many states, the maximum is set by law as a percentage of the average wage in the state. All states now provide potential duration of UI for at least twenty-six weeks, with a few states providing more time. Qualification requirements vary from state to state. In a few states, all who qualify are entitled to the same number of weeks of benefits. In most states, however, benefit duration depends on your base period of work and wages.

Federal unemployment taxes on employers finance this benefit. Two states — Alaska and New Jersey — also tax employees for this purpose, and two states — Pennsylvania and West Virginia — receive employee contributions under certain conditions.

WHO IS ELIGIBLE?

1. Those who are unemployed through no fault of their own — that is, through layoffs, company or plant closing, and natural disasters — are eligible. This means that you did not quit your job, although there are exceptions to this as well.

2. Some states might allow for UI if you have left your employer because working conditions were so bad they would cause any "reasonable" person to quit. If you have questions, consult a lawyer.

3. In order to qualify for UI, you must be able to work and be available for suitable work. You must register for work with the employment service and otherwise be actively seeking work in most states.

4. If you have elected the Cobra plan, you will not be considered a company employee, and you thus can collect UI. The

Cobra plan is federal legislation mandating that a company must permit a former employee to stay on health benefits for eighteen months, past the end of their termination or severance package date. If you elect the Cobra plan, you must pay the whole bill. Noninterrupted health insurance is the primary benefit of Cobra.

WHO IS NOT ELIGIBLE?

1. In most states, you would be prohibited from collecting UI if you were fired for deliberate misconduct or willful disregard of the employer's interests.

2. All states disqualify those who voluntarily quit without good cause.

3. Those who are self-employed do not qualify.

4. If you have not worked a minimum amount of time, you will not qualify for benefits.

5. Striking workers generally do not receive UI.

6. If you refuse, without good cause, an offer or referral to suitable work, you will not receive UI.

7. Eligibility for UI is tied to whether or not you are receiving benefits. If you are receiving benefits *paid for by the organization,* you are still considered an employee and thus, in most instances, not eligible to collect UI.

Check with your state's employment security agency for details, or consult with a plaintiff employment attorney.

Employment Services

WHAT ARE THEY?

Every state provides free "employment services" to all workers, out of work or not. Services differ from state to state and can include support groups, vocational/career counseling, workshops (resumé writing, networking, interviewing), job development, an automated directory of statewide jobs, and job placement.

Important: Receiving UI does not automatically register you for employment services. You must register for unemployment services separately. Do this when you apply for UI. At some point in your transition, these services could be beneficial to you.

WHERE ARE THEY?

The name of each state's employment security agency differs (for instance, Department of Employment and Training in Massachusetts, Employment Security Commission in Mississippi, and Employment Development Department in California). In addition, specific employment services — workshops, support groups, automated directories of jobs — vary from state to state. The following is a national listing of state employment security agencies and their telephone numbers:*

ALABAMA, Department of Industrial Relations, 205-242-8990
ALASKA, Employment Security Division, 907-465-2712
ARIZONA, Department of Economic Security, 602-542-5678
ARKANSAS, Employment Security Department, 501-682-2121
CALIFORNIA, Employment Development Department, 916-654-8210
COLORADO, Department of Labor and Employment, 303-837-3801
CONNECTICUT, State Labor Department, 203-566-4384
DELAWARE, Department of Labor, 302-577-2713
DISTRICT OF COLUMBIA, Department of Employment Services, 202-639-1000
FLORIDA, Department of Labor and Employment Security, 904-488-4398
GEORGIA, Georgia Department of Labor, 404-655-3011
HAWAII, Department of Labor and Industrial Relations, 808-586-8844
IDAHO, Department of Employment, 208-334-6110
ILLINOIS, Department of Employment Security, 312-793-5700
INDIANA, Department of Employment and Training Services, 317-232-3270
IOWA, Department of Employment Services, 515-281-5365
KANSAS, Department of Human Services, 913-296-7474

*This list and other benefits information in this section were taken from *Highlights of State Unemployment Compensation Laws* (Washington, D.C.: National Foundation for Unemployment Compensation and Worker Compensation, January 1992).

KENTUCKY, Department of Employment Service, 502-564-5331

LOUISIANA, Department of Employment and Training, 504-342-3011

MAINE, Bureau of Employment Security, 207-289-2411

MARYLAND, Department of Economic and Employment Development, 301-333-5070

MASSACHUSETTS, Department of Employment and Training, 617-727-6600

MICHIGAN, Michigan Employment Security Commission, 313-876-5500

MINNESOTA, Department of Jobs and Training, 612-296-3711

MISSISSIPPI, Employment Security Commission, 601-961-7400

MISSOURI, Division of Employment Security, 314-751-3976

MONTANA, Department of Labor and Industry, 406-444-3555

NEBRASKA, Department of Labor, 402-471-3405

NEVADA, Employment Security Department, 702-687-4635

NEW HAMPSHIRE, Department of Employment Security, 603-228-4000

NEW JERSEY, New Jersey Department of Labor, 609-292-2323

NEW MEXICO, New Mexico Department of Labor, 505-841-8409

NEW YORK, New York State Department of Labor, 518-457-2270

NORTH CAROLINA, Employment Security Commission of North Carolina, 919-733-7546

NORTH DAKOTA, Job Service North Dakota, 701-224-2836

OHIO, Bureau of Employment Services, 614-466-2100

OKLAHOMA, Employment Security Commission, 405-557-7200

OREGON, Employment Division, Department of Human Resources, 503-378-3208

PENNSYLVANIA, Department of Labor and Industry, 717-787-1745

PUERTO RICO, Bureau of Employment Security, 809-754-5394

RHODE ISLAND, Department of Employment and Training, 401-277-3732

SOUTH CAROLINA, Employment Security Commission, 803-737-2617

SOUTH DAKOTA, Department of Labor, 605-773-3101

TENNESSEE, Department of Employment Security, 615-741-2131

TEXAS, Texas Employment Commission, 512-463-2652

UTAH, Department of Employment Security, 801-536-7401

VERMONT, Department of Employment and Training, 802-229-0311

VIRGINIA, Virginia Employment Commission, 804-786-3001

VIRGIN ISLANDS, Department of Labor, 809-773-1440

WASHINGTON, Employment Security Department, 206-753-5114

WEST VIRGINIA, Bureau of Employment Programs, 304-348-2630

WISCONSIN, Department of Industry, Labor and Human Relations, 608-266-7552

WYOMING, Employment Security Commission, 307-235-3200

Unemployment Insurance and Social Security

There is a common confusion that UI and Social Security (SS) are one and the same. *They are not!** UI is employer funded. Every worker is *not* eligible. UI is temporary income, intended as a means of support if you have lost your job, usually through no fault of your own.

SS is funded by you when you work in a job covered by Social Security. During your working years, you receive SS earnings credits. These credits are used later to determine your eligibility for SS retirement benefits or for disability or survivors' benefits if you should become disabled or die.

You can receive SS for the following reasons:

- you have retired
- you have become disabled
- you are dependent on someone who receives SS
- you are a widow, widower, or child of someone who has died

Depending on your circumstances, you may be eligible for SS at any age. For more information call the Social Security Administration at 1-800-772-1213 between 7 A.M. and 7 P.M. every business day.

---

*The source of information on Social Security is *Understanding Social Security,* SSA Publication no. 05-10024 (Washington, D.C.: Social Security Administration, U.S. Department of Health and Human Services, January 1992).

Who to Go to for Help

Partially stimulated by the proliferation of job loss throughout the world, resources for dealing with job loss and finding another job abound. Resources fall into the categories of books, periodicals, and directories; support groups and agencies (profit and nonprofit and federal, state, and private); specialists (counselors, psychologists, and consultants); universities and associations; and colleagues, friends, and family. For many, the number of choices, and who or what to use and when, can be overwhelming.

The following information is intended to guide you toward the best "human resources" appropriate to the particular stage of your transition. First, some common and useful human resources are defined; then, when to use them and for what are clarified.

Human Resources

Career counselor. A professional who helps a client understand what she or he is thinking and feeling and why she or he is acting in a particular manner. Career counselors can help you understand the job marketplace and explore various industry sectors, changes in your profession, and potential occupations. Furthermore, they will guide you in understanding how to enter, survive, and enhance your career and advance in your profession in the marketplace and workplace. They can help you change professions, if that is what you desire, and will help you sort out, identify, and prioritize your skills, values, interests, and ambitions. Then they will aid you in matching your personal qualities to the characteristics of the marketplace. Finally, they will coach you through the interviewing and decision-making process.

Deliverables:* support through listening; career testing of skills, values, beliefs, interests; coaching on how to focus, how to write

Deliverables refer to the professional services you can receive from each resource. The deliverables mentioned are *not* a comprehensive list; there are others. In addition, deliverables can overlap in professional areas. For example, a career counselor, outplacement consultant, and counseling psychologist might all contribute "insights" but may go about the counseling process differently.

a resumé as well as marketing and cover letters, how to network and interview, how to implement a mid-career change, and how to follow action planning methods.

   Lawyer. When you've lost your job, a lawyer will help you understand and act on your rights. If you have questions about unfair practice, meet with a lawyer to explore the issues. Ask about the fee *before* you meet. For example, ask, "Is there a fee for the first meeting?" and "What can be expected out of the first meeting?" As mentioned earlier, you should choose a plaintiff employment lawyer, one who represents the employee, not management. Many who lose their jobs have doubts about their rights or are intimidated by large companies — namely, their ex-employers. It will take moral courage to face your former employer; you don't have to do it alone. If you have questions about fair practice, *first* find out from a lawyer if you have a legal issue or not.
   Deliverables: letter of reference (sometimes not provided by ex-employer); securing of unemployment benefits and status as a paid employee while you look for another job if you are entitled to these; help keeping your personnel files confidential and ensuring a fair agreement as to why you left the company.

   Counseling psychologist. A licensed professional who can help you take a whole-life perspective, incorporating family issues, internal and external expectations, psychological blocks, personal ambitions, and marketplace contingencies when making career and life choices. Counseling psychologists can have a specialty in career-related concerns and/or work in conjunction with a career counselor. Some career counselors also take a whole-life perspective. Like career counselors, many career psychologists have found that their clients' problems are a result of not being able to make an appropriate career choice or to find a job.
   Deliverables: support through listening and encouragement to talk about feelings; psychological and career testing; guidance on how to combine work and family life; development of long- and short-term career and life goals; insights about reasons for making choices; advice on how to go from insight to action.

Outplacement consultant. Outplacement consultants are professionals hired by a client company to counsel ex-employees at all levels who have been dismissed from their jobs. Dismissal usually includes layoff, early retirement, or an agreed-on parting of the ways. Outplacement consulting is a half-billion-dollar industry that has been fueled by rampant industry layoffs. Most outplacement consultants work for outplacement firms. Outplacement counseling, as a rule, is a resource that is paid for by an employer. If this service is not provided by your former employer, call a local or international outplacement firm and ask them for a career counselor referral in your area. *The Directory of Outplacement Firms,* put out by Kennedy Publications, is a national listing of these firms. The directory provides information, including company name, address, and telephone and description and strengths of the firm. The cost is $74.95 plus $6.00 postage and handling. Call 1-800-531-0007 or ask for this directory at your local library.

Deliverables: support through listening and encouragement to talk about feelings; coaching on how to uncover skills, write a resumé, uncover leads, and negotiate salary; advice about the job marketplace and how to job hunt.

National and international firms can provide office services and office space for the purposes of job hunting; computerized national and international job bank; networking with other job seekers from the same and different industries; and a worldwide historical network.

Two international outplacement/human resource consulting firms are: Drake Beam Morin, Inc., Outplacement and Human Resource Consulting, 100 Park Avenue, New York, NY 10017, 212-692-7700 (57 offices nationally, 60 offices internationally); and Right Management Consultants, Career Transition and Human Resource Consulting, 1818 Market Street, Philadelphia, PA 19103-3614, 800-237-4448 (73 offices nationally, 14 offices internationally, 8 offices in Canada).

University career counselor. Many universities and colleges provide counsel, workshops, and career testing for alumni and nonalumni. Their rates are typically reasonable, ranging, for example, between $30.00 and $45.00 per hour for career counseling. Many of these facilities also have information and career resource libraries that are updated frequently.

Deliverables: counsel on defining interests, skills, and values; books, pamphlets, and articles on careers and career issues; financial aid and grant information; videotaped practice interviews; local job listings.

Support group. A support group can range in size from two to two hundred members, or more. In the past three or four years, many groups focused on helping those who have lost their jobs have developed across the United States. Generally, these groups are well organized, support people at *all* levels, and provide self-help management and workshops on career change, skill evaluation, interviewing, networking, and marketing. Some, such as WIND, which is located in the Boston area (508-475-2742), provide specialized networking groups and weekly speakers who share their expertise on timely topics. Some groups charge a nominal fee, but often there is no charge. For a support group in your area, refer to the "Calendar of Events" in the *National Business Employment Weekly,* or call your local state employment security agency.

Deliverables: support and validation for feelings (you are not alone); a place to go on a weekly/biweekly basis (a "meeting" to go to); new ideas, especially what has and hasn't worked for others; job-search skill development; job leads.

Leaderless support group. The purpose of a leaderless support group is to help every member gain mastery and identify and accomplish his or her goals. Ideally, a leaderless support group involves four to six members who meet in one another's homes. Meetings are based on guidelines developed by the group. (For other guidelines, refer to page 92 (box).)

Deliverables: support (you can do it); constructive criticism (you are on or off track or need to do more research); new ideas; networking beyond known contacts; interview practice through role playing.

Placement specialist. A professional who matches the employment needs of corporate clients with talent in the marketplace.

Placement specialists usually work on a contingency basis; they are paid by the client company contingent on finding the right person for a particular position. Most placement professionals have their areas of specialization, such as computer programming, compensation and benefits, human resources, or marketing and sales. Some fill many types of positions but focus on particular industry sectors, such as health care, biotechnology, or retail.

Deliverables: jobs in desired area of specialization; advice about resumé presentation, interviewing, and salary negotiation; knowledge about professional areas represented.

Search consultant. Like placement specialists, search consultants also match the employment needs of their corporate clients with talent in the marketplace. However, they typically work on an exclusive consulting contract basis with the client company and often get paid whether they fill the position or not. Many search consultants make it their job to form close relationships not only with the client company, but also with professionals, usually mid- to upper-level, with whom they network and place. The *Directory of Executive Recruiters,* updated annually, provides information—name, address, contact person, and brief description—of contingency and noncontingency firms. Information is cross indexed by management function, industry, and geography and is geared to the independent job seeker. Available through Kennedy Publications, the cost is $39.95. Call 800-531-0007 to order.

Deliverables: high-level jobs; in-depth information about client companies; advice about interviewing and salary negotiation.

Colleagues and associates. The people you know can be very supportive and helpful. Call someone you've worked with recently or someone from your distant past. Choose someone you trust, someone who will listen. Tell your story. At a different stage in your transition, such as networking, former colleagues and associates can be excellent sources. They will have ideas, know other contacts, and possibly direct you to job leads.

Friends and family. Some family members and friends can be very supportive; others, for various reasons, will turn away. Learn to shed the criticism and choose family and friends who listen, not judge; who are patient and want to help you problem solve; who have faith and can help you see that things will get better; and who share their own feelings.

Choosing Helpful Resources

Selecting the resource that will be most helpful to you in your career/job change depends on your transition stage. The stages that follow when you lose your job are:

Stage 1: *Confusion*—you have lost your job.

Stage 2: *Story Telling*—talking about your feelings and what happened.

Stage 3: *Getting on Track*—clarifying and prioritizing skills, values, and interests.

Stage 4: *Networking*—expanding options and discovering opportunities.

Stage 5: *Focusing*—targeting and researching industry sectors, companies, and opportunities.

Stage 6: *Interviewing*—selling yourself.

Stage 7: *Evaluation*—deciding which opportunities would be best for you.

Stage 8: *Negotiating*—working out a fair compensation package.

Stage 9: *Beginning Again*—deepening your learning, enhancing your career, and contributing to your new situation.

After you lose your job, the transition stages that follow *are not linear.* Progress is rarely up and forward. Rather, you can expect to *go back and forth* between stages in a seesaw motion. For

Choosing Helpful Resources

Transition Stages

Resources	Confusion	Story Telling	Getting on Track	Networking	Focusing	Interviewing	Evaluation	Negotiation	Beginning Again
Career Counselor	●	●	●		●		●	●	●
Lawyer	●							●	
Counseling Psychologist	●	●							●
Outplacement Consultant		●	●	●	●	●	●	●	
University Career Counselor		●	●	●	●	●	●	●	
Support Group	●	●	●	●	●				
Leaderless Support Group				●	●	●	●	●	●
Placement Specialist				●		●		●	
Search Consultant						●	●	●	
Colleagues/Associates		●		●	●	●			
Friends/Family	●	●	●	●					

example, many people experience confusion when they first lose their jobs (stage 1); it is also common to feel confused as you sort out your feelings (stage 2) and when you are deciding which companies to target (stage 6)—the choices can be overwhelming. Also, you could start a new job (stage 9) and still feel some confusion as to whether you made the best choice. Even though these stages are intertwined, as you persevere, you will progress from one stage to the next.

In addition, you will use skills you've developed in one stage and perfect them in other stages. For example, throughout your transition you will hone your analytical skill, beginning with analyzing your feelings (stage 2). You will also analyze your skills and values (stage 3) and analyze the fairness of your compensation offer (stage 8). Your transition will proceed in fits and starts, but don't be discouraged. This time provides an opportunity to enhance your skills, self-knowledge, and awareness of the vast marketplace of work opportunities. The preceding table can help in selecting resources appropriate to your transition stage.

Section C
Services

Services include places you can go — support groups, agencies, workshops, and associations — for support, information, and skill development if you've lost, or anticipate losing, your job. Following is detailed information on six distinct services available nationally:

Forty Plus is a nonprofit organization for experienced executives, managers, and other professionals over forty years old who are in career transition.

Operation A.B.L.E. is a nonprofit association that promotes employment opportunities for individuals forty-five and older and provides networking, counseling, job-search training, and professional skills training.

Exec-U-Net is a professional networking group that provides job leads and job-search counsel.

Dialog is a computerized data base that can be used for gathering information on industry sectors and/or specific complaints.

Johnson O'Connor Research Foundation is a nonprofit educational organization with two primary commitments: to study human abilities and to provide people with a knowledge of their aptitudes that will help them in making decisions about school and work.

American Association of Retired Persons is a nonprofit, nonpartisan organization dedicated to helping older Americans achieve lives of independence, dignity, and purpose.

For other services, refer to the Calendar of Events published weekly in the *National Business Employment Weekly,* a *Wall Street*

Journal publication. This is an excellent job-search reference and career help guide. For career guidance, also take special note of the articles featured. The purpose of the Calendar of Events is to publicize events and services for job seekers that are either free or of nominal cost. The support groups and events publicized are national, including Alaska, Hawaii, and Canada. For quick access they are divided into four regions. To subscribe, call 800-JOB-HUNT (562-4868).

Forty Plus

This is a national, nonprofit organization for experienced executives, managers, and other professionals over forty years old who are in career transition. There are twenty North American chapters. Forty Plus benefits include career workshops, support groups, unadvertised job listings, networking with current members and alumni (1,500 +), and weekly professional speakers. Contact information for the twenty chapters follows:

NORTHERN CALIFORNIA

Forty Plus of Northern California
7440 Lockheed Street
(P.O. Box 6639)
Oakland, CA 94603-0639
510-430-2400
FAX 510-430-1750

Forty Plus—South Bay Division
1250 Aviation Avenue, Suite 175
San Jose, CA 95110
408-288-3555
FAX 408-288-3563

SOUTHERN CALIFORNIA

Forty Plus of Southern California
3450 Wilshire Boulevard, Suite 510
Los Angeles, CA 90010
213-388-2301
FAX 213-383-7750

Forty Plus—Orange County Division
23172 Plaza Pointe Drive, Suite 285
Laguna Hills, CA 92653
714-581-7990
FAX 714-581-4257

SOUTHERN CALIFORNIA (*continued*)

Forty Plus—Orange County
Chapter
San Diego Office
4715 Viewridge Avenue,
Suite 200
San Diego, CA 92123
619-278-5355
FAX 619-278-5989

COLORADO

Forty Plus of Colorado
393 South Harlan Street
Lakewood, CO 80226
303-937-6668
FAX 303-937-6050

Forty Plus—Northern Division
3842 South Mason Street
Fort Collins, CO 80525
303-223-2470 (ext. 261)
FAX 303-223-7456

Forty Plus—Southern Division
2555 Airport Road
Colorado Springs, CO 80910
719-473-6220 (ext. 271)

DISTRICT OF COLUMBIA

Forty Plus of Greater
Washington
1718 P Street, N.W.
Washington, DC 20036
202-387-1582
FAX 202-387-7669

HAWAII

Forty Plus of Hawaii
126 Queen Street, Suite 227
Honolulu, HI 96813
808-531-0896

ILLINOIS

Forty Plus of Chicago
28 East Jackson Boulevard
Chicago, IL 60604
312-922-0285
FAX 312-922-4840

NEW YORK

Forty Plus of Buffalo
701 Seneca Street
Buffalo, NY 14210
716-856-0491
FAX 716-852-2292

Forty Plus of New York
15 Park Row
New York, NY 10038
212-233-6080
FAX 212-227-2974

OHIO

Forty Plus of Central Ohio
1700 Arlington Lane
Columbus, OH 43228
614-275-0040

PENNSYLVANIA

Forty Plus of Philadelphia
1218 Chestnut Street
Philadelphia, PA 19107
215-923-2074

TEXAS

Forty Plus of Dallas
13601 Preston Road,
Suite 301 East
Dallas, TX 75240
214-991-9917
FAX 214-991-9932

Forty Plus of Houston
2909 Hillcroft, Suite 400
Houston, TX 77057
713-952-7587
FAX 713-952-8829

UTAH

Forty Plus of Utah
5735 South Redwood Road,
Room 207
Salt Lake City, UT 84123
801-269-4797
FAX 801-269-4708

WASHINGTON

Forty Plus of Puget Sound
300 120th Avenue, N.E.,
Bldg. 7, #200
Bellevue, WA 98005
206-450-0040
FAX 206-450-9631

TORONTO, CANADA

Forty Plus of Canada
920 Yonge Street, Suite 410
Toronto, Ontario
Canada M4W 3C7
416-366-6766

Operation A.B.L.E.
(Ability Based on Long Experience)

This is a nonprofit organization that promotes employment opportunities for individuals age forty-five and older who represent
economically, racially, and occupationally diverse populations.
Founded in 1982, Operation A.B.L.E.'s mission is accomplished
through the provision of employment and training services, advocacy, and collaboration with public agencies and the business
community.

There are eight independently operated A.B.L.E. affiliates across
the country:

ARKANSAS

Arkansas A.B.L.E.
Phyllis Haynes,
  Executive Director
519 E. Capitol Avenue
Little Rock, AR 72202
501-374-1318

CALIFORNIA

L.A. Council on Careers for
  Older Americans
Sally E. Jones,
  Executive Director
5225 Wilshire Boulevard,
  Suite 204
Los Angeles, CA 90036
213-939-0391

ILLINOIS

Operation A.B.L.E., Inc.
Shirley Brussell,
  Executive Director
36 South Wabash Avenue
Chicago, IL 60603
312-782-3335

MASSACHUSETTS

Operation A.B.L.E. of
  Greater Boston
Ruth Ann Moriarty,
  Executive Director
119 Beach Street, 4th Floor
Boston, MA 02111
617-542-4180

MICHIGAN

Michigan Project A.B.L.E.
Terry Barclay,
  Executive Director
17330 Northland Park Court
Southfield, MI 48075
313-442-0370

NEBRASKA

Operation A.B.L.E. of S.E.
  Nebraska
Jacque Haisch,
  Executive Director
129 N. 19th Street, Room 332
Lincoln, NE 68508
402-471-7064

NEW YORK

N.Y.C. Dept. for the Aging
Senior Employment Service
Richard J. Braun,
  Executive Director
2 Lafayette Street, 15th Floor
New York, NY 10007
212-577-7595

VERMONT

Vermont Associates for
  Training and Development
Pat Elmer,
  Executive Director
P.O. Box 107
St. Albans, VT 05478
802-524-3200

Exec-U-Net

This is a cooperative of senior executives who have leveraged the concept of individual networking into a unique member-driven organization. Every two weeks, the network publishes its job opportunity listings with base salaries of $75,000 and above. The network accepts information on nonadvertised openings only. Regional meetings are held monthly, and a newsletter on career management is published quarterly. The network currently supports human resources, finance, information systems, legal, sales, marketing, operations, and general management. Membership is nationwide and confidential. The fee is $75.00 for a three-month period, or $300.00 per year. For more information, contact Exec-U-Net, 21 November Trail, Weston, CT 06883, 203-226-5710/ FAX 203-226-7881.

Dialog Information Services, Inc.

Dialog is an on-line information service. Dialog gives you a means to turn raw data into useful knowledge and insight and enables you to find the answer to specific questions. For example, Dialog can provide you with the answer for this question: "What are the names of the presidents of biotech firms in California and New England having fifty employees or more?"

By connecting your PC to Dialog, you can quickly scan a variety of documents, including press releases; company directories; financial data; local and international newspapers; worldwide patent, trademark, and copyright information; and more. This information is drawn from respected information providers, including Dun & Bradstreet, Standard & Poor, McGraw-Hill, Associated Press, and Financial Times. Dialog has offices throughout the United States and the world. Call Dialog marketing with your questions at 800-3-DIALOG (800-334-2564).

If the company you're leaving has access to Dialog, you may want to negotiate the use of the system as a portion of your severance package. In addition, ask your outplacement counselor if his or her firm has access to this system.

Johnson O'Connor Research Foundation

The Johnson O'Connor Research Foundation has been included as a resource because the service they provide, aptitude testing, can lead to your discovering your natural talents. One way to make progress in your transition and to find *meaningful* work is to discover your aptitudes. Aptitudes are natural talents — special abilities for doing, or learning to do, certain kinds of things easily. Your aptitudes, like the color of your eyes, hair, and skin, are inherited. Musical and artistic talent are examples of aptitudes.

The primary purpose of taking aptitude tests is to reveal the areas in which you have ability. It has been the foundation's experience that people tend to be more satisfied and successful in occupations that challenge their aptitudes and do not demand aptitudes that they lack.

The Johnson O'Connor aptitude testing program assists you in discovering the course of study and the type of work that will fit your aptitude pattern. They will help you understand why certain courses of study and occupations are likely to be more satisfying or rewarding than others. As Johnson O'Connor, the founder, put it many years ago, "The individual who knows his [her] aptitudes, and their relative strengths, chooses more intelligently among the world's host of opportunities."

Johnson O'Connor has eleven offices across the United States. They use the name "Johnson O'Connor Research Foundation" for all their offices, with the exception of Boston, which still uses the original name, "Human Engineering Laboratory." Following is contact information for the eleven Johnson O'Connor offices:

ATLANTA
3400 Peachtree Road, N.E.
Atlanta, GA 30326
404-261-8013

CHICAGO
161 East Erie Street
Chicago, IL 60611
312-787-9141

BOSTON
347 Beacon Street
Boston, MA 02116
617-536-0409

DALLAS/FORTH WORTH
5525 MacArthur Boulevard
Irving, TX 75038
214-550-9033

DENVER
One Cherry Center
501 S. Cherry Street
Denver, CO 80222
303-388-5600

HOUSTON
3200 Wilcrest
Houston, TX 77042
713-783-3411

LOS ANGELES
3345 Wilshire Boulevard
Los Angeles, CA 90010
213-380-1947

NEW YORK
11 East 62nd St.
New York, NY 10021
212-838-0550

SAN FRANCISCO
The Monadnock
685 Market Street
San Francisco, CA 94105
415-243-8074

SEATTLE
1218 Third Avenue
Seattle, WA 98101
206-623-4070

WASHINGTON, D.C.
201 Maryland Avenue
Washington, DC 20002
202-547-3922

American Association of Retired Persons

Founded in 1985, the American Association of Retired Persons (AARP) is today the nation's oldest and largest organization of older Americans, with a membership of more than 33 million. Membership is open to anyone age fifty or older, both working and retired. Over one-third of the association's membership is in the work force. Membership dues (including spouse) are $8.00 for one year, $20.00 for three years, and $45.00 for ten years. Dues for those outside U.S. domestic mail limits are $10.00 per year or $24.00 for three years. For further information, contact AARP Communications Division, 601 E Street, N.W., Washington, DC 20049, 202-434-2560.

AARP members receive bimonthly the nation's most widely circulated magazine, *Modern Maturity,* and the *AARP Bulletin* eleven times a year. The association also distributes a wide range of specialized publications, many of which are available free of charge in limited quantities on request. Three examples are:

Look Before You Leap: A Guide to Early Retirement Incentive Programs.
The mergers, takeovers, corporate restructuring, and downsizing of the last decade have prompted many companies to offer their older employees enticing incentives to take early retirement. If you've taken an early retirement or are thinking about it, this publication will answer some important questions.

Age Discrimination on the Job. The federal Age Discrimination in Employment Act (ADEA) protects most workers age forty and older from discrimination on the job. The ADEA is based on an important policy and fact: that ability, not age, should determine an individual's qualifications for getting and keeping a job. This publication reviews discriminatory actions covered by the ADEA.

A Woman's Guide to Pension Rights. Because many women rely heavily on their husband's pensions, and because most women outlive their spouses, women have traditionally suffered most when pension benefits are unavailable. This brochure deals only with private and union pension plans. It will tell you what your basic rights are and suggest questions to ask either the person administering the plan, your attorney, or someone specializing in pension rights.

Other membership services of AARP include group health insurance, automobile/homeowners insurance, mobile home insurance, investment program, Visa card program, travel program, travel and leisure values, pharmacy service, educational resources, community service, criminal justice services, health advocacy services, health care campaign, and work force programs.

Section D

Assessment Inventories

Assessment inventories in this section are of two types: self-administered and counselor-administered. These materials are inventories, not tests; their purpose is to give you useful information, not a letter grade. These inventories are intended to help you learn about yourself and the work world. They cannot match you with the perfect job, but they can help you identify the interests, values, needs, and beliefs important in your career choice and fulfillment. What you learn will help you to find meaningful work.

Self-Administered Tools

Career Anchors: Discovering Your Real Values, by Edgar H. Schein.

Available through University Associates, Inc., 8517 Production Avenue, San Diego, CA 92121, 619-552-8901. (Order two books, because the "Career Anchor Mutual Interview" requires you to have a partner and each will need a copy.)

According to the introduction of this book and self-diagnostic guide, "A career anchor is a person's self-image of what he or she excels in, wants, and values. This book is designed to help you determine your career anchor and to think through your career options." The author goes on to say, "You may wonder why it is important to know your career anchor. When you confront career choices, it is important to make those choices in a manner consistent with what you *really* value. Your career anchor reflects the pattern of factors that you really do not want to give up, because they represent your *real* self."

A career anchor is similar to a career theme (discussed on pages 138–39 in the text). I recommend this book and diagnostic instrument primarily because it fosters independence and responsibility. In the words of Dr. Schein, "You will learn about those motives and needs, talents and skills, and personal values that you would not give up if you were forced to make a choice." By knowing what is important to you, you'll be able to make better choices and articulate more clearly what you want to do and what you can do for an organization or a customer. In a word, *self-management* is central to your career success. *Career Anchors* will bring you a giant step closer to "taking charge."

Counselor-Administered Tools

Described below are three counselor-administered tools. The *Strong Interest Inventory* measures your *interests* (not your skills or aptitudes) in a range of activities — work, school, leisure — and compares them to those of individuals in over one hundred occupations. The results can suggest fields that will be most compatible with your interests. The *Career Beliefs Inventory* can help you understand those career *beliefs* that may be preventing you from achieving your goals. The *Myers-Briggs Type Indicator* will give you an understanding of your personality type, which can help you choose your career.

Strong Interest Inventory, by Edward K. Strong, Jr.

Available through Consulting Psychologists Press, Inc., 3803 East Bayshore Road, Palo Alto, CA 94303, 800-624-1765.

The *Strong Interest Inventory* (the *Strong*) has been in use since 1942. It continues to be thoroughly researched and is a valid and reliable instrument. The *Strong* is an inventory of interests that have nothing to do with skills and natural talents. By taking the *Strong,* your career counselor can help you (1) define and clarify your interests, (2) suggest career areas for exploration, and (3) guide leisure and retirement planning. This inventory takes about thirty minutes to complete. You should count on one to three counseling sessions for interpretation, feedback, and planning.

Career Beliefs Inventory, by John D. Krumboltz

Available through Consulting Psychologists Press, Inc., 3803 East Bayshore Road, Palo Alto, CA 94303, 800-624-1765.

The *Career Beliefs Inventory* (CBI) will help you uncover those beliefs that can interfere and those that can facilitate the accomplishment of your career goals. In the words of the author, "The way in which people make career decisions, search for jobs, and seek promotions depends on what they believe about themselves and the world of work. If their beliefs are accurate and constructive, they will act in ways that are likely to foster the achievement of their goals. If their beliefs are inaccurate and self-defeating, they will act in ways that make sense to them but may hinder accomplishments of their goals." With the aid of a career counselor or outplacement consultant, the CBI can be administered and used as a springboard for a healthier career transition. To purchase this test, you must have satisfactorily completed a course in the interpretation of psychological tests and measurement at an accredited college or university.

Some people who lose their jobs *believe* that "it's the end of the world," or that "they'll never find a decent job again," or that "it's most important to satisfy my spouse's needs over my own" or that "I can't learn a new skill." As long as you are believing these things, you will be living these things. Taking the CBI is a way to identify what you believe and to examine what you can do about changing those beliefs that are getting in the way of your progress.

Myers-Briggs Type Indicator (MBTI), by Isabel Briggs Myers

Available through Consulting Psychologists Press, Inc., 3803 East Bayshore Road, Palo Alto, CA 94303, 800-624-1765.

The MBTI, in the words of Isabel Briggs Myers, "is concerned with valuable differences in people that result from the way they like to perceive and the way they like to judge. Succeeding at anything takes both perception and judgment. First, you have to find out what the problem or situation is and what are the various things you might do about it. Then you have to decide which to do. Finding out is an exercise of perception. Deciding is an exercise of judgment."

This instrument and Myers's book, *Introduction to Type,** can help you determine your type, and thus give you additional information useful in choosing among careers/jobs that will give you a chance to use your *own combination of perception and judgment*. For example, one type, INFJ (Introverted, Intuitive, Feeling, Judging) is described by Paul D. Tieger and Barbara Barron-Tieger, specialists in the use of the MBTI, as follows:

> *Brief Personality Description:* Quietly forceful; motivated by inspiration and inner vision, which they value above all else; trust their ideas in the face of skepticism and persevere in seeing them applied and accepted; and have strong desire to contribute to the welfare of others.
>
> *Interpersonal Style:* Empathic; aware of others' emotions and interests and deal well with complex people; seek harmony in interpersonal relationships; prefer to agree with others and are troubled by conflict; and share inner selves only with those they trust.
>
> *Environmental Considerations:* Need smooth running, conflict free environments; opportunities to better the world; need time to concentrate and formulate ideas; do well working alone; and need opportunity to prepare thoroughly.
>
> *Vocational Preferences:* Good organizational skills; take their work seriously; not often visible leaders — great workers behind the scenes; need their work to reflect their perfectionism; sometimes able to compose great works of art; enjoy working with others, but prefer a one-on-one basis; use language well — enjoy writing professions; enjoy problem solving, and using systems creatively.
>
> *Vocational Functions:* These are *some* occupations which may offer this "type" potential for satisfaction: social worker, novelist, psychologist, career counselor, human resource manager, and marketer.

*Isabel Briggs Myers, *Introduction to Type* (Gainesville, FL: AMSA Foundation, 1978).

Section E

Books, Directories, and Periodicals

Books and Directories

Getting a Grip on Things: Job Loss Management

Your Rights in the Workplace, by Dan Lacey (Berkeley, CA: Nolo Press, 1991).

This is a comprehensive factual guidebook to your rights on the job — from hiring through firing. It covers issues from illegal firing and layoffs; wages and overtime; sex, race, and age discrimination; and how to challenge job loss.

Before you contact an attorney, you may want to see what this book has to say about the issue that concerns you. By taking the initiative to educate yourself first, if you then decide to hire an attorney, you'll be making an educated choice and most likely will save time and money.

Job Bank Guide to Employment Services, edited by Giselle deGuzman and Cathy Corbett (Holbrook, MA: Bob Adams, Inc., 1989).

This guide contains detailed information on over 3,200 career counseling and resumé writing services, executive search firms, and employment agencies/temporary help services throughout the United States. Employment service profiles contain all the information necessary to target firms best able to satisfy a job seeker's needs: firm name, address, telephone number; contact person; area of specialization; common job categories filled; special programs and workshops offered; and fee policy. Three separate geographical/specialization cross indexes make this book a powerful tool for locating specialized employment services in other geographical areas.

Employment service guides like this one can be helpful resources for those who have lost their jobs and have not been provided with outplacement counsel or access to other forms of career assistance, those who need help expanding their search into other geographical areas, those for whom personal or professional referrals are not available, and those feeling the need to expand their networks.

Being Peace, by Thich Nhat Hanh (Berkeley, CA: Parallax Press, 1987).

The author, a monk of over forty years born in central Vietnam in the mid 1920s, became actively engaged in helping victims of the war and in communicating their message for peace. This book is an outcome of his 1985 lectures to peace workers. In the words of the editor, Arnold Kotler, "Thich Nhat Hanh's teaching provide a crucial antidote to our busy lives."

Being Peace offers the rich yet so often neglected and difficult (especially in our Western culture) perspective of living in the moment. Many who have lost their jobs add more anxiety to their fears by living primarily in the future, worrying, for example, that "if I can't find a job like the one I had, then I can't be fulfilled" or "I'll go broke even though I've been given a year's severance." The author comments that such future thinking leads essentially to not living, at least not in the present: "'I have to wait until I have a job in order to be *really* alive.' And then after the job, a car. After the car, a house." He goes on to say, "We may never be alive at all in our entire life. Therefore, the technique, if we have to speak of a technique, is to *be* in the present moment, to be aware that we are here and now, and the only moment to be alive is the present moment." Hanh believes that losing one's job can be an opportunity for rebirth, a beginning to live in the moment.

Coming to Terms with Job Loss and Managing Transition

When Smart People Fail: Rebuilding Yourself for Success, by Carole Hyatt and Linda Gottlieb (New York: Penguin Books, 1987).

This is a very *real* account of the authors' own experience and more than 150 case histories of the famous — Walter Cronkite, Polly Bergen, and Geraldine Ferraro — and the not-so-famous. These case studies support the authors' practical, positive advice on how to cope with failure and some of the tools for rebounding.

Transitions: Making Sense of Life's Changes, by William Bridges (Reading, MA: Addison-Wesley, 1980).

This book puts change into a natural and realistic context — as a part of life. This is an insightful guide "for coping with the difficult, painful, and confusing times in your life," including times of personal as well as career crisis. The author takes his reader step by step through the transition process — "endings, the neutral zone," and "the new beginning" — offering suggestions and advice.

Parting Company: How to Survive the Loss of a Job and Find Another Successfully, by William J. Morin and James C. Cabrera (New York: Harcourt Brace Jovanovich, 1991).

This is an informative, detailed text with practical exercises for those who have lost their jobs. The authors' practical advice is supported by several case studies, questions, checklists, and worksheets. The authors are, respectively, the chairman and the president of Drake Beam Morin, Inc., world leaders in outplacement consulting.

What Smart People Do When Losing Their Jobs, by Kathleen A. Riehle (New York: Wiley, 1991).

For many, grappling with the feelings associated with job loss is immense; this book helps. This is not a "how to" guide to job searches or résumé writing. The content is tailored to the specific situation of someone currently out of work and looking for a new position. It is practical, covering issues such as financial planning and applying for unemployment insurance.

Writing the Natural Way: A Course in Enhancing Creativity and Writing Confidence, by Gabriele Lusser Rico (New York: Jeremy P. Tarcher, Inc., 1983).

The title for chapter 1 says it all: "A Book That Will Release Your Inner Writer." One way to "tell your story" throughout your career transition is to write. Keep a personal journal and, when you get a job, keep a business journal as a way to see yourself as productive, to release your feelings, to review what does and doesn't work, and to keep track of your progress. This book will help guide your self-expression through writing.

Developing a Positive Attitude and Taking Responsibility

Oh, the Places You'll Go! by Dr. Seuss (New York: Random House, 1990).

This book offers advice in rhyme for proceeding in life; weathering fear, loneliness, and confusion; and being in charge of your actions. In the words of Dr. Seuss:

> You have brains in your head.
> You have feet in your shoes.
> You can steer yourself
> any direction you choose.
> You're on your own. And you know what you know.
> And YOU are the guy who'll decide where to go.

There are many books that address the theme of change and being in charge of your actions, but unlike many, Dr. Seuss gets to the heart of the matter and to *your* heart. His writing is compassionate, compelling, and concise. This book will hit home and save you time; why read a three- or four-hundred page book when Dr. Seuss will get you there sooner?

The Seven Habits of Highly Effective People: Powerful Lessons in Personal Change, by Stephen R. Covey (New York: Simon & Schuster, 1990).

This is a personal leadership handbook that teaches the reader not only how to achieve external success, but also that which is much more elusive for many—inner success. For those who have lost their jobs, this book will affirm some of your effective habits and will give you insights into and how to develop others.

Assessing Your Beliefs, Interests, Skills, and Values

What Color Is Your Parachute? A Practical Manual for Job-Hunters and Career Changers, by Richard Nelson Bolles (Berkeley, CA: Ten Speed Press, 1993).

Now in its twentieth year in print, this book is a classic in career literature. Bolles offers time-tested insights and methods for self-evaluation, including how to assess your beliefs, interests, skills, and values. The author humorously helps you put your findings to use, advocating that you uncover the "hidden job market."

The New Quick Job-Hunting Map: How to Create a Picture of Your Ideal Job or Next Career, by Richard Nelson Bolles (Berkeley, CA: Ten Speed Press, 1992).

In Richard Bolles's words, "In order to hunt for your ideal job, or even something close to your ideal job, you must have a picture of it, in your head. The clearer the picture, the easier it will be to hunt for it. The purpose of this booklet is to guide you as you draw that picture."

Finding the Right Job for You: How to Do It

Do What You Love, The Money Will Follow: Discovering Your Right Livelihood, by Marsha Sinetar (New York: Dell, 1987).

For many in this time of change, a primary concern is selecting work that is fulfilling. Sinetar focuses on paying attention to your inner wisdom as you progress through job transition and find your next job. This book is for those who are looking for more than money out of their work. In the words of the author, this is a "handbook that hopefully will show readers 'how' to follow their own hearts to the work of their dreams. And more: it is at its core a comment about the spiritual aspects of work—a book that suggests people can fulfill themselves as authentic, unique human beings through doing their right livelihoods."

This philosophy is borne out in real life. For example, on July 29, 1992, NBC television aired the *Fortune* 400 profiles of some of "the richest people in America." Those interviewed advised out-of-work people to "find out what you really like doing, focus on it, and you'll achieve success."

The Encyclopedia of Careers and Vocational Guidance,
edited by William E. Hopke (Chicago:
J. G. Ferguson Publishing Company, 1990).

This directory is divided into four volumes: I—Industry Profiles, II—Professional Careers, III—General and Special Careers, IV—Technicians' Careers. Volume I, Industry Profiles, gives information on a broad range of industry categories, ranging from advertising and agriculture, to marketing and motion pictures, to health care and retailing, to printing and recording, to telecommunications to waste management. Volumes II, III, and IV give information on specific occupational categories, including actors and actresses, architects, commercial artists, data base managers, fundraisers, groundwater professionals, pilots, school administrators, therapists, and writers.

The information in each category is comprehensive. Within each occupational category, you will find the following: definition, history, nature of work, requirements, special requirements, opportunities for experience and exploration, related occupations, methods of entering, advancement, employment outlook, earnings, conditions of work, social and psychological factors, and sources of additional information.

This directory can be found in your local library. It is a low-risk method of networking, although it does *not* replace networking with people. A source that can give you an overview and a range of specific information about a variety of industries and occupational areas, it can be used to gain information before and after you go on informational and job interviews.

Wishcraft: How to Get What You Really Want, by Barbara Sher with Annie Gottlieb (New York: Ballantine Books, 1979).

In the words of the authors, this book is "designed to make you a winner. Winning," authors say, "means getting what you want. Not what your father or mother wanted for you, not what you think you can realistically get in this world, but what *you want* — your wish, your fantasy, your dream. You're a winner when you have a life you love, so that you wake up every morning excited about the day ahead and delighted to be doing what you're doing, even if you're sometimes a little nervous and scared."

When you've lost your job, you can feel not only a little nervous but also very scared. Part of your challenge is to turn your anxiety and fear into learning and ultimately make your dream come true. Job loss is an opportunity to begin again, to venture out to get what you want. Many wonder if people find what they really want to do after losing a job. The answer is yes, they do — but only if they take full responsibility and make it happen.

Directory of Executive Recruiters (Fitzwilliam, NH: Kennedy Publications).

Published annually and listing over 2,000 executive recruiter firms, this directory can be reviewed at your public library or can be ordered by calling 800-531-0007.

Finding the Right Job for You: Where to Look

America's Fastest Growing Employers: The Complete Guide to Finding Jobs with over 700 of America's Hottest Companies, by Carter Smith (Holbrook, MA: Bob Adams, Inc., 1992).

The author provides an all-in-one national career guide for those seeking employment with the most rapidly growing companies in the country. From high-tech or entrepreneurial start-ups to *Fortune* 500 giants, all firms profiled here are on the fast track of the American economy. Included are companies such as Wal-Mart, Gateway 2000, Birmingham Steel, Banyan Systems, and Sunrise Medical. This book provides names, addresses, and vital statistics of over 700 companies; an overview of the company's products and services; and reasons the company is growing rapidly.

You can use this resource to work smarter, not harder by adopting a "silver-bullet," not a "scatter shot," approach. This is how. First, target three companies that interest you in a desired geographical area. Next, call the marketing departments in each company for additional information—annual reports, brochures, special service and product information. If you're working with an outplacement firm, use the telephones there to save on long-distance calls. To deepen your learning, while you're waiting for this information to arrive (1) ask friends, colleagues, and associates for additional information about these companies and (2) do further research in your local library. Then, write each of these three companies a special marketing letter. Remember, write to the top—the highest-ranking person who has the responsibility for the area of the organization that interests you. Finally, follow through by calling your company contact to further introduce yourself and to discuss how your background and expertise might suit the company's needs. If there is some compatibility, be bold—ask for a meeting. You've got everything to gain.

Jobs 92: A Complete Sourcebook for All Job Hunters and Career Changers, by Kathryn Petras and Ross Petras (Englewood Cliffs, NJ: Prentice-Hall, 1992).

This book offers leads on more than 40 million jobs and how to get them. It is a great resource guide to help you find the work you want.

The National Job Bank 1990, edited by Carter Smith (Holbrook, MA: Bob Adams, Inc., 1990).

Available in your local library, this job bank directory is national in scope, providing employment contact information for thousands of companies. You can also purchase *Job Bank* directories that target specific metropolitan and geographical areas across the country.

When using this directory, try targeting the smaller business market (SBM), those companies that have fewer than 2,500 employees. Some of these companies may be growing from a new venture "cowboy" stage into a "professionalization" stage. Some of the tasks in SBM companies might include clarification of job descriptions, financial planning, management training, and policies for customer-oriented shipping and receiving. If you've worked at a larger company, you will have a desirable background and expertise, which you can "sell" to a growing SBM. It is important to first learn to speak the "language" of the SBM before you write your marketing letter or go on your interview. For example, in a larger organization you may have had a "marketing" title and function. In the SBM, marketing is "sales." The SBM is concerned with how you can help develop and make sales, not with marketing.

Good Works: A Guide to Careers in Social Change, 4th ed., edited by Jessica Cowan (New York: Barricade Books, 1991).

If you think you might be interested in social change work, this book can be a useful resource. It will provide you with profiles of people engaged in full-time citizen work, listings of organizations, and a compilation of resources and networks. Organizations listed with detailed information range from the American Lung Association in New York, to the Center for Maximum Potential Building Systems in Texas, to the Institute for Social Justice in Arkansas.

Writing Resumés and Letters

The Perfect Resumé, by Tom Jackson (New York: Doubleday, 1990).

This comprehensive book provides worksheets and up-to-date resumé examples, including suggested resumé formats such as the chronological resumé, functional resumé, targeted resumé,

resumé alternative, and creative alternative. You will also find easy-to-use resumé drafting forms and salary negotiation strategies.

Cover Letters That Knock'em Dead, by Martin Yate (Holbrook, MA: Bob Adams, Inc., 1992).

This book is filled with examples and advice on how to write a "knock'em-dead" cover letter.

The Perfect Cover Letter, by Richard H. Beatty (New York: Wiley, 1989).

This is a how-to guide, with examples that include cover letter formats and characteristics of good and poor cover letters.

Interviewing

Sweaty Palms: The Neglected Art of Being Interviewed, by H. Anthony Medley (Berkeley, CA: Ten Speed Press, 1992).

This is a terrific resource—a thoroughly informative and practical book that covers such interview topics as preparation, enthusiasm, nervousness, dress, salary, discrimination, decisions, commonly asked questions, and "turnoffs."

Knock'em Dead with Great Answers to Tough Interview Questions, by Martin Yate (Holbrook, MA: Bob Adams, Inc., 1992).

This is another excellent guide that covers the hidden job market, how to handle any interview situation, salary negotiations, responses to illegal questions, and information on how to respond if you're asked to take a drug test.

Learning: Going to School

Comparative Guide to American Colleges, by James Cass and Max Birnbaum (New York: HarperCollins, 1991).

This directory can be found in your local library and contains the following: detailed information on admissions; current educational cost; scholarships and loans; majors; and religious, racial, and ethnic composition of the student body.

For those that have lost their jobs, there is not just one option, but many. Often, when one chooses and stays on a course and keeps one's eyes and ears open along the way, an opportunity will present itself. Going to school part- or full-time can be a choice that leads not only to self-renewal, but also to the advancement and enhancement of your career.

The Graduate Scholarship Book, by Daniel J. Cassidy (Englewood Cliffs, NJ: Prentice-Hall, 1990).

This book offers a complete guide to scholarships, fellowships, grants, and loans for graduate and professional study. It can be found in your local library.

Free Money for Graduate School: A Directory of Private Grants, by Laurie Blum (Troy, MO: Holt, Rinehart & Winston, 1990).

This is the first comprehensive book to provide all known sources of private monies available for furthering your education. Wherever possible, the author has included the total amount of money awarded to students, the number of grants given, the average size of an award, and the range of monies given.

America's Lowest Cost Colleges: A Comprehensive Directory of More Than 1,000 Fully-Accredited Colleges and Universities with Low or No Tuition, by Nicholas A. Roes (Barryville, NY: NAR Publications, 1991).

According to the Department of Education, if you made a list of the fifty best colleges and universities in the nation, there would be as many low-cost public schools on the list as high-priced private ones. Categorized alphabetically by state, the names, addresses, and phone numbers in this directory provide the information you need to send or call for a catalog. Also, tuition is listed for a full academic year. This is a small, manageable book, 115 pages in length.

Going Beyond: When You Have a Job

The Age of Unreason, by Charles E. Handy (Boston, MA: Harvard Business School Press, 1990).

This is a book about making sense of our changed times. In the words of the author, "The book is addressed primarily to those who work in and who manage organizations or some part of them, because it is their hands that rest on the levers of change. . . . The changes which we are already seeing in our lives, and which we see more of, have their origins in the changes in our workplaces."

In today's world, organizations, profit and nonprofit, have many questions and they're looking for answers. One question is "How do we gain competitive advantage?" There are few simple answers to these questions, but there are answers. It is the responsibility of everyone who has lost a job or who has a job to provide the answers—that is, to add value to the customer and/or an organization—and to raise other questions. Handy shares some valuable historical, present, and future perspectives for looking at the world, including what some organizations have done to go beyond survival and how some of his principles, such as the "inverted doughnut" (mentioned in the text on pages 181–82), can be used and applied. Handy reminds us to "look change in the face and see it for what it is—an opportunity as well as a challenge." This resource will give you global and personal insights and can also help you to win—an employer or a customer.

The Fifth Discipline: The Art and Practice of the Learning Organization, by Peter Senge (New York: Doubleday, 1990).

So many products and services are simply replications of each other. How do the hundreds and thousands of organizations producing these goods and services not only survive, but also distinguish themselves and thrive in a global marketplace? According to Senge, developing a learning organization is the new source of competitive advantage. In his words, "Learning disabilities are tragic in children, but they are fatal in organizations. Because of them, few corporations live even half as long as a person—most die before they reach the age of forty." By overcoming these learning disabilities, organizations and the people in them can thrive.

For both those who have lost their jobs and those currently earning a paycheck, this book can stimulate you to go beyond your current experience in your thinking and actions. As you network for a job or network within your own company, try talking about the principles underlying "the learning organization." What may be perceived as "learning disabilities" in many instances can be viewed as "under-par abilities."

The Road Less Traveled: A New Psychology of Love, Traditional Values and Spiritual Growth, by M. Scott Peck (New York: Simon & Schuster, 1978).

At a time when self-esteem is low, as it often is with job loss, Scott Peck can help put the journey called life in perspective. He raises our consciousness and suggests taking full responsibility for our lives, but he also reminds us about balance — "the capacity to reject responsibility that is not truly ours." He discusses other issues, such as "openness to challenge, the healthiness of depression, and the work of attention."

The first line in this book is "Life is difficult." The third line tells us that this is "a great truth because once we truly see this truth, we transcend it." Job loss for most is difficult, but for those who face the difficulties, paradoxically, the hardships become challenges. As Peck suggests, we have a remarkable ability to make choices. In this case, to turn job loss, a label given to a set of circumstances, into opportunity.

In today's marketplace and workplace, people talk about going back to traditional values — education, family, hard work, and saving money. It is likely that these values were never gone, but only buried temporarily under rapid growth, technological advancement, and greed. These times are requiring us to make conscious, balanced choices. You will gain an inner security and at the same time enhance your career and life by reexamining and prioritizing your values. This is a book that can aid in that process.

Mindfulness, by Ellen J. Langer (Reading, MA: Addison-Wesley, 1989).

In *Mindfulness,* Langer teaches us about being more aware and awake—more alive. She says, "When we are mindful, we are open to surprise, oriented in the present moment, sensitive to context, and above all liberated from the tyranny of old mindsets." In today's marketplace and workplace, there is no room for being "on automatic." This book offers liberating alternatives to "there's only one way."

The eighth chapter of this book, "Mindfulness on the Job," reminds us that old mindsets can result in "fatigue, conflict, and burnout." Similarly, old mindsets can also lead to the same symptoms when you're *looking* for a job.

Periodicals

Commonplace magazines and newspapers are often overlooked as valuable up-to-date resources. These publications can address several needs—for example, they can validate your feelings, give you an overview and specific details about the economy, share survival tactics as times change, and recommend job-search techniques that have worked for others. In addition, many articles are authored by individuals who can be excellent sources for information networking. Call or write them. You may discover a vital link to your next job. Since your journey will have many beginnings, magazines and newspapers will continue to apprise you of changes and innovative ideas. Some key periodicals include:

National Business Employment Weekly

This publication was mentioned earlier in the services section. It is the *Wall Street Journal*'s weekly summary of nationwide job opportunities and combines a week's worth of help-wanted advertisements from all areas of the *Wall Street Journal.* To subscribe, call 800-JOB-HUNT (562-4868) or purchase a copy at a newsstand for $3.95.

Wall Street Journal

This newspaper, published daily by Dow Jones & Company, is an excellent source for marketplace trends, information on finance and small and large businesses, and *ideas.* To subscribe, call 1-800-841-8000, ext. 276.

Inc.: The Magazine for Growing Companies

This monthly magazine includes articles such as "How to Succeed without a Job," "Inc.'s Guide to Creating Your Own Workplace in the '90s," and "Fast Rising: A Start-up Founded by Laid-off Workers." To subscribe, call 1-800-234-0999.

Business Week

Published weekly, except for one issue in January, this periodical includes articles such as "I'm Worried About My Job!" and "A Career Survival Kit for the 90's." To subscribe, call 1-800-635-1200.

Fortune

Published biweekly, with three issues in May and October, this periodical has articles on such topics as "The New Executive Unemployed." To subscribe, call 1-800-621-8000.

Author's Note

Whether you've just lost your job or you're ready to go beyond, I want to wish you well by sharing this quote from poet/novelist Rainer Maria Rilke:*

> I want to beg you, as much as I can, to be patient toward all that is unsolved in your heart and to love the *questions themselves* like locked rooms and like books that are written in a very foreign tongue. Do not now seek the answers, which cannot be given you because you would not be able to live them. And the point is, to live everything. Live the questions now. Perhaps you will then gradually, without noticing it, live along some distant day into the answer.
>
> Resolve to be always beginning — to be a beginner!

*Rainer Maria Rilke, quoted in *Rilke on Love and Other Difficulties,* ed. John J. L. Mood (New York: Norton, 1975), 25.

Index